ABOUT THE BOOK

"How did I become an impersonator? Perhaps my mother was conceived by a Zerox machine!"

So, how did a kid from Ottawa, Canada, growing up in the '50s become an impressionist? No one in our family had ever been in show business. No one ever had "show biz" yearnings. My father was a doctor. My mother was a housewife. So where did my desire to become an impressionist come from? I've often asked myself this question. I didn't know the answer, but I did love the movies. As a boy, I would go every weekend, sometimes staying to see the show twice. Just going to the movies and getting so involved in the story-telling and the characters made me want to be that person up on the screen, never dreaming that I could turn it into a career.

The glory days of Hollywood and their icons, like no other, have remained as indelible images in our hearts and minds for decades. I, like many, idolized these giants of the screen and comedy, but was so fortunate to have had the opportunity to meet, work with, and get to know many of them along the way during my career. From the genius of Jack Benny, the unmatched humor of George Burns, the debonair, handsome Cary Grant, the unforget-table John Wayne, the king of late night hosts Johnny Carson, and the former actor-turned-president Ronald Reagan to name a few.

In this gem of a book are insights into the likes of many of these great people I've had the privilege and fortune to meet and imitate, shining new light on our beloved stars.

This is really not a biography, but more of a humorous glimpse of the people I've impersonated and some of the funny stories that happened along the way.

"Little by Little"
(People I've Known and Been)

by
Rich Little

First published by Dog Ear Publishing
4011 Vincennes Rd
Indianapolis, IN 46268
www.dogearpublishing.net

ISBN: 978-1-4575-4439-2

This book is printed on acid-free paper.

Printed in the United States of America

Acknowledgements

There are many people to thank for making this book a reality. First and foremost, my beloved Marie, who worked tirelessly to make sure my story was written, and Jeri Fischer who worked by her side.

My gratitude to Annie Linderman (one of my biggest fans) who worked on the original manuscript and final rendition; Charlotte Morgante for her initial research; Denci Freeri for his hours of photo restoration; and Dāna Stern for her input, research, editing, and final preparation for publishing.

Special thanks to my dear friends Gord Atkinson and Ray Stone for their foreword and afterword, as well as their many insights and suggestions.

Finally, thank you to the wonderful subjects of this book, without whom my career would not have been possible.

Epigraph

"The best form of flattery is to be admired,
imitated or respected. There's a sense of
pride knowing others look up
to us or feel we are inspirational."

Table of Contents

FOREWORD

One of my closest friends is a friend of legendary stars and prominent politicians. He is indeed the alter ego of the famous personalities of our time. He is also the entertainment world's most popular impressionist/comedian. We have been pals for 60 years!

Rich Little has raised the gift of mimicry to an art form. His impressions are so accurate and so amazing that he has recorded movie soundtrack dialogue for ailing stars without the public realizing they were listening to his voice.

Rich grew up in the family residence, which was at a choice Ottawa location on the scenic driveway that parallels the historic Rideau Canal. I first met him when he was a high school cut-up and I was hosting a radio show for teenagers, "The Campus Club." He made his showbiz debut on that program in the fall of 1956.

The brilliant impressionist from Canada's capital honed his gift for mimicry doing take-offs of his teachers' voices. As he recalls with humor, "There was a concentrated campaign among the faculty to graduate me early – with or without a diploma."

It was at this time that he perfected one of his most famous voices. A James Stewart western was a box-office hit and had a lengthy Ottawa run. All that summer, at every opportunity, he would ask his mother (in the familiar drawl of Jimmy Stewart) for a 'piece of apple pie.' He considers that voice at that time as being the benchmark of his unique career.

Although the Little family had no theatrical background, Rich had a solid and thorough training as an actor during his formative years. He has high praise for the guidance and experience he gained at the Ottawa Little Theatre, where he appeared in both dramatic and comedic roles. "Everything I know about acting was developed from those early years," he says with affection.

Ottawa's perennial showbiz son has received the "key to the city" twice, had a day proclaimed in his name during an official homecoming, and had a street named in his honor. In January 1992, he was acclaimed again at a testimonial dinner for disadvantaged children by the Variety

Club of Ottawa. He has also been feted for his charitable work by another theatrical institution, The Friars Club, in both New York and Los Angeles.

The recipient of entertainment and humanitarian awards, Rich gives freely of his time and talent for worthy causes, and has raised millions of dollars for charitable events. The profits from his unforgettable, hometown concert with Frank Sinatra in 1982, built the "Rich Little Special Care Nursery" at the Ottawa Civic Hospital. "That was one of the high water marks of my life and career," he proudly states.

Through the persistent efforts of one of his earliest supporters, Mel Tormé, Rich made his American TV debut on *The Judy Garland Show* in 1964. Tormé was a musical consultant and a frequent co-star on that program. The Little guest spot was so electrifying, that overnight, Rich became the most sought-after performer in show business, sharing the spotlight on variety shows with his boyhood comedy idols Jack Benny, George Burns and Bob Hope.

When a Little impression is being developed, he will work on the subject with the aid of a tape recorder to perfect his impersonation. "Sometimes it can take me months to develop a difficult voice," Rich admits, "while other times I'll duplicate a more obvious voice in a matter of minutes. The singing voices are my greatest challenge. It's strange, but when I sing like Robert Goulet, for example, I can hit notes that are beyond my normal range."

Rich is a modern day impressionist of both voice and form. His pen and ink portraits are amazing lifelike images of his fellow performers and friends. The money from the sale of his sketches (as with his other merchandise) is distributed to the families of wounded warriors in both Canada and the US.

Rich doesn't do impersonations in normal conversation today as he did years ago. However, now and then he will catch someone off guard on the phone and try to convince them that he is someone else. Early in our friendship, this was a common occurrence. "Like a caricaturist, I exaggerate the speech pattern and quality of a person's voice and magnify their mannerisms." Incidentally, Rich's incredible collection of over 200 voices includes a devastating impression of yours truly.

In September 2013, Rich returned to the stage of his theatrical roots, the Ottawa Little Theatre, performing his greatly acclaimed tribute to his boyhood hero and close friend James Stewart. Written, directed and performed by Rich, *Jimmy Stewart & Friends* is an amazing tribute to the iconic actor featuring a Little tour de force of the "voices" of famous Hollywood stars.

★ ★ ★ ★

It was our mutual fascination with show business and show people that first brought Rich and me together as friends and showbiz buffs. I also share with him a tendency to be forgetful. Here are a few embarrassing examples:

An intense moment occurred prior to the arrival of Frank Sinatra for the Sinatra-Little million-dollar Ottawa concert. As we awaited his arrival by private jet, we shared intense moments of nervous energy. Rich suddenly turned to me and said with panic in his voice, "Gee, I hope I gave him the right date!"

Travelling with Rich is always an adventure. We have been lost more times than multiple episodes of the television drama *Lost*. Driving along the Los Angeles freeways can be intimidating and confusing – especially if you don't concentrate on where you are going. For example, there was the time when we followed a car with a big dog looking out the back window. We thought we were following our wives and the Little's sheep dog on our way to visit friends. By the time we realized we were following the wrong car with a look-alike sheep dog, we were hopelessly lost. It took several phone calls for directions and a St. Bernard rescue dog to help us find our way!

On another occasion, we were running late in the same car for separate interviews. I was on my way for an interview with a prominent recording artist and Rich was scheduled to attend a meeting at The Beverly Hills Hotel. Needless to say, while distracted by spirited conversation, we missed both appointments. Once again, we were lost in the "City of Angels." At a critical moment, Rich looked at me and said nervously, "Where are we?" To which I replied defensively, "How should I know? I don't live here." He retorted in a moment of geographic confusion, "Well, you should, you're here often enough!"

Once when flying to Los Angeles from Las Vegas, I found myself among an all-star passenger list. On board were Orson Welles, Eddie Albert, Red Buttons, Jimmy Stewart and Rich. As we flew over the stark foreboding desert, Rich leaned over to me and said, "Do you realize that if this plane should crash, your name won't even be mentioned. And even if you are identified, they will probably misspell your name!"

Our mental missteps and escapades were an unintentional throw-back to those zany Laurel and Hardy comedies – that always ended with the inevitable line by Oliver Hardy to Stan Laurel, "Well, that's another fine mess you've gotten me into!"

★ ★ ★ ★

In 1984, Rich took me to the Beverly Hills home of Jimmy and Gloria Stewart where he had arranged for me to do an in-depth radio interview with the legendary star. I began our taped conversation by reminding Mr. Stewart that Rich had often said that the voices he does best are the voices of the people he admires the most. And there was no one Rich admired more than Jimmy Stewart – his boyhood movie idol.

"The feeling is mutual," Stewart replied, "I have great admiration for Rich. He is a master of his craft. He does my voice and mannerisms so well, that people now tell me that I remind them of Rich Little."

"There's No Business Like Show Business," and no show like a Rich Little comedy concert with a cast of countless famous voices both past and present!

Gord Atkinson
Ottawa, Ontario, Canada

"Little by Little"
(People I've Known and Been)

All sketches (giclees) in book done by Rich Little

Will the Real Rich Little Please Stand Up?

My father:
Lawrence Peniston Little

My mother:
Elizabeth Wilson Little

*H*ow did a kid from Ottawa, Canada, growing up in the '50s become an impressionist? No one in our family had ever been in show business. No one had ever had "show biz" yearnings. My father was a doctor, a urologist. My mother was a housewife. So where did my desire to become an impressionist come from? I've often asked myself this question. Sure, my mother acted in a couple of plays when she was a young lady. But my father, a man of great kindness, with solid religious values, had no interest in show business whatsoever – except that he admired Jack Benny and George Burns. And, he loved to go to the movies.

I was the second of three sons. My brothers, Fred and Chris, had no idea what they wanted to do with their lives when they were young boys. As a matter of fact, I don't think they ever did! And I must admit that at an early age, I didn't know either. But I did love the movies. My mother took me to my first film. I can't remember what it was – probably a "grown-up" movie, because I fell asleep. I remember being fascinated with the actors and the movement on the screen, and it wasn't long before I was going to the movies every weekend. My brothers and I, each with twenty-five cents or so in our pockets, would set off to the Rialto Theater or the Imperial Theater to see a double-feature every single weekend. We watched either a cowboy movie or some kind of action-adventure film, and we never missed a week. At the Rialto – which we called the rat-hole – you could see a movie for fifteen cents. It was a terrible place. We didn't know if it had rats or not, but we put our feet up on the seats in front of us just in case. Looking back, I doubt if there were really rats. It was just a crummy, dismal little theater; but it was cheap, and they showed a lot of cowboy movies. Red Ryder, the Cisco Kid, Allan "Rocky" Lane, Monte Hale, Roy Rogers, Tim Holt – all the cowboy heroes of my childhood flashed across the screen.

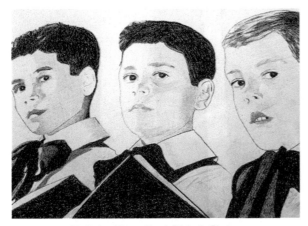

Little brothers: Fred, Rich & Chris -
Three angelic choir boys

Those were the days of the double bill – two movies, plus a newsreel, previews, and a cartoon. Sometimes, we'd sit through the show twice, which meant that if we went to the noon show, we wouldn't get home until five or six o'clock. I was never worried about getting a spanking for being out so late, because I'd been sitting in the theater so long my bottom was already numb! We just loved watching the action, and when the good guy was pursuing the bad guy, riding after the stagecoach, or shooting at the villains, you could've heard a pin drop. But when the heroine appeared, or if there were any kind of love scenes, or – yuck! – kissing, we'd talk among ourselves until our hero jumped back onto his horse. Then we'd be dead quiet again.

After the show we'd come home and play cowboys and Indians, or swashbuckling pirates. There was a vacant lot behind our home covered with trees and bushes. It was very rugged in some spots, so it was the perfect place to act out our Westerns or sword-fighting films. Someone had made us some wooden swords – I don't remember who – but they had handles and seemed very real. We'd play on that vacant lot until we dropped. I already had a very vivid imagination, and those films allowed my imagination to run riot.

A babbling youth at 5

Long before I started to do impressions, I'd get up in front of the class and tell stories. It started when I was in kindergarten. I'd just babble on and on, with nothing prepared, no structure to my story, no ending, no punch line. I made it all up with such enthusiasm and such excitement and drama that the kids were mesmerized. I had a flair for the dramatic from the get-go.

I was a bit of a loser as a kid. I was clumsy and a bit of a nerd. I seemed to be the brunt of many jokes. I think my first impression was of Inspector Clouseau. One Saturday, Fred, Chris and I were on our way to the Rialto (about five or six blocks from our home), when we came upon a pit-bull. It was growling at us and wasn't tied up. I said to my brothers, "I'm going home, or I'm going to find another way to the theater. There's no way I'm walking past that dog. It's going to bite us." But my oldest brother Fred said, "Not necessarily. If you show the dog you have no fear and just ignore it, act superior, and walk right by, the dog won't bite you." I said, "I dunno. That dog looks pretty vicious to me." So, Fred put on kind of an air and walked right past the dog. Then Chris did the same thing. And, in Clouseau fashion, I put my nose in the air and marched past the dog just as they had. The dog bit me, and I had to get a tetanus shot! Yes, I think that was my very first impression.

Although my brother Chris and I were close most of our lives, when we were younger, around twelve or thirteen, we fought a lot, and he was always trying to beat me up. The school bully was a French kid named Jacques Pelletier. He really was a mean kid. One day when we were playing on a vacant lot, I went after Jacques, because I was mad at him for some reason. I picked up a huge rock and yelled, "Jacques, I'm going to knock you out with this rock." He yelled back, "Oh, no you're not!" He then grabbed my brother Chris around the throat. "You will

"BONES" LITTLE

Basketball player Lawrence Little
at McGill University

Lt. Commander Lawrence Little in the
Canadian Navy

not throw that rock, because you'll hit your brother. I'm using him as a shield." I evaluated the situation. I decided he was lying. I threw the rock. I knocked my brother out cold. He was unconscious for about two minutes. My father finally brought him around with some smelling salts. Jacques growled at my father, "Doesn't your son know what a shield is?"

Apart from the fact that Chris and I fought all the time, our family was fairly normal. We were a very loving family. There were no drugs, and no one drank very much. Very occasionally, my father got a little tipsy when he went to a party, but I never saw him really drunk. My mother was the disciplinarian. I guess she won that role by default.

Chris and I sometimes started fighting with knives in the attic and continued all the way down to the basement. It's a miracle that neither of us got stabbed. Chris really was the athlete of the family. He was a great footballer. I tried out for football, but wasn't particularly good at it, nor was my brother Fred. So, I became a cheerleader. That was more my style. Plus, there were a couple of gorgeous girls on the cheerleading squad, and that really appealed to me.

Chris took after my father, who was a true athlete and excelled at anything that had to do with sports or games of skill. He was a smart card player, and loved to play darts. We had a dartboard in the basement, and my dad nailed one bulls-eye after another, while the rest of us just hit the wall, the

My dad: Navy days

Doctor Little

A young Elizabeth Wilson Little

sink, the boiler – anywhere but the dartboard. The basement looked like a graveyard for darts.

My dad was a doctor in the Navy with the rank of Lieutenant Commander. He was often away at sea and was the doctor for the entire convoy; he went from ship to ship whenever anyone needed medical assistance. It was a pretty dangerous job. When the tides were high, he had to know exactly when to grab the net and swing up onto the deck, because two seconds later the boat would drop fifty feet. He really loved the Navy. I don't think he saw much combat, but he loved the ocean, and he loved the solitude of being at sea. When we lived in Halifax, Nova Scotia, we'd all troop down to see dad off. He'd get into a little boat and row out to one of those huge ships. Without fail, I'd turn to my mother and say, "There he goes! We'll never see him again!" Yep, I was a real bundle of joy in those days.

My dad had an excellent reputation as a skilled surgeon, but after the war, he gave up his practice to work for the government as a medical consultant. I know he spent much of his time wondering if he'd made the right decision, but I don't think he could take the pressure of people dying anymore. It used

Mum with a very young me doing my first impression of Ronald Reagan

to prey on his mind a great deal. I don't think he was really happy working for the government, but he loved his family and he knew that he had to put food on the table. He was always in great shape; he walked three miles to and from work every day. But he had one vice – he smoked too much. I guess smoking was his downfall, because he was only sixty years old when he died. But he was an extraordinary man. He wrote poetry. In fact, I found a book of about 40 or 50 poems that he'd written for my mum when they were younger. They were beautiful. I can honestly say that I loved my dad dearly.

Of course, I loved my mum too. She was very social and quite pampered. We had a lady come and clean for us two or three times a week. Dad made sure mum was taken care of. She was always the disciplinarian. She ran the show. If we boys were fighting, she would take care of it. My dad hated to be the bad guy – he just couldn't handle it. Once, my mother insisted he come upstairs to stop us kids from screaming. He ran up and immediately started to spank me – didn't even take the time to pull down the bed sheet. He never realized that he didn't hurt me. I'd stuffed a magazine down my pajama pants. After my dad died, my mum became my biggest fan. She came to all of my shows and sat in the front row, however, if I ever said anything slightly off-color – like when I was doing Jack Nicholson – she'd just get up and leave. Her body wore out at 94, but not her mind. The last thing she ever said to me was, "Don't wear that brown suit on *The Ed Sullivan Show*."

It was my dad who took me to the first grown-up movie. It was 1951, and I was about 13 years old. The film was *A Christmas Carol*. Dad said, "I hope you understand this is not a Western." I was so excited about going to the movies with my dad and seeing a real, grown-up movie, I said, "No, no

– I'll be fine." And I was. Seeing Alastair Sim as Scrooge at the Elgin Theater in Ottawa was a huge turning point in my life. From that day on, I forgot all about cowboy movies.

The thing about seeing *A Christmas Carol* as a kid is that the story was very easy to follow. It's basically about a man who is a very evil skinflint. When three spirits visit him on Christmas Eve to show him what a mean and miserable man he is, he changes his life. That simple. I was fascinated by it and have loved Alastair Sim ever since. It's been filmed many times, but I don't think there's ever been a version as good as that 1951 black and white one. It's a true classic. The story stayed in my head, and I eventually read the book by Charles Dickens. It took a while, but I managed to get through it.

From then on, I went to more grown-up movies. The kids would say, "Hey, we're going to the Rialto to see Allan "Rocky" Lane." And I'd say, "No, no, no! I'm going to the Elgin [or the Capitol] to see Jimmy Stewart!" Or it might have been John Wayne or Humphrey Bogart. They'd say, "What? That stuff's boring!" Well, it wasn't boring to me. That's how I started to really appreciate good acting and how I got to know a lot of stars. And I wanted to be like them.

That's when this whole idea of being an impersonator came into my head, slowly, without my realizing it. Just going to the movies and getting so involved in the storytelling and the characters that I wanted to

My partner Geoff Scott and me

be that person up there on the screen, never dreaming that I could turn that into a career.

Almost every day, I hung out with my friend Geoff Scott. We had the same interests. We'd draw cartoons and comic books, cut out pictures of our favorite stars and make scrapbooks – things like that. While Chris and Fred were still going to the Rialto, Geoff and I would go to the more sophisticated Capitol. And then, without really realizing what we were doing, Geoff and I started imitating what we saw on the screen. We'd sword-fight like Errol Flynn; we'd talk with a lisp like Humphrey Bogart; we'd walk with a swagger like John Wayne. We couldn't really do the voices yet, but we did our damndest to be like the guys we saw on the screen.

Alan Ladd

Our favorite actor was Alan Ladd. When we saw *Shane*, sometime around 1954, we were really hooked. *Shane* was the perfect movie for a kid with an imagination, because it was about a boy who idolized a gunfighter and wanted desperately to be like him. And, the kid actually ends up saving the life of the gunfighter. We'd try to be like Alan Ladd – strong, silent and soft-spoken. Geoff had an advantage, because he was fair-haired. We'd cut out any picture of Alan Ladd we could find in any magazine and we each had an Alan Ladd scrapbook. I still have mine today. It's a bit dog-eared, but I love to look through it and conjure up many happy memories.

When I heard that Alan Ladd was coming to Ottawa, Geoff and I went absolutely nuts. He had been making a picture with Shelly Winters in Saskatchewan, called (cleverly) *Saskatchewan*. He was coming to Ottawa to do some looping (voice dubbing), although I don't know why they didn't do this back in California. He was doing it at Crawley Films; they had top-notch facilities and were pretty well known in Canada, even though they specialized in documentaries. When Geoff and I heard that Alan Ladd was going to be at Crawley Films on a Monday morning, we were down there like lightning, first in line at six in the morning. I had with me a picture I'd drawn of Alan Ladd – I don't have it any more, but I can still remember what it looked like. It came out pretty well.

By nine o'clock, there were about 50 or 60 people in line behind us. Finally, Alan Ladd arrived. He stopped in front of us. I showed him my picture, and he asked, "Did you really draw this?" I stammered, "Yes sir, I did." And he said, "Very, very good. What's your name?" I said, "Rich." And he signed the picture, "To Rich. Good luck, Alan Ladd." That was a *really* big deal for me, and I never forgot it. Today, when I see kids waiting at the stage door, I try to picture myself doing this with Alan Ladd or with a few other stars when I was keen to meet them as a kid.

Going back to *A Christmas Carol* for a moment…this marked the beginning of my love for British films. There's nothing I love more than watching a British movie on a rainy night in front of a blazing fireplace. And I love British actors. The accent has never bothered me at all. I saw so many of them as a kid; I can watch them today and understand every single word, including Cockney and all the regional dialects. There was a theater in the west end of Ottawa that showed nothing but British movies. I'd go there every weekend for a double bill – they all seemed to star Alex Guinness or Trevor Howard or Jack Hawkins or John Mills. The '40s was a great era for British films, when Ealing Studios and J. Arthur Rank were turning out between thirty and forty films a year. Unfortunately, it pretty well came to an end in the late '50s.

Here's a story that's the flip side of the Alan Ladd story. It deals with Richard Todd, a British actor – not huge – who had made quite a few movies in the '40s and then filmed *Rob Roy* and *Robin Hood* for Disney. In 1955, he made a picture called *The Dam Busters*, which was the story of Dr. Barnes Wallace. Wallace invented a prototype bomb that skipped on the water and blew up a slew of dams in the Ruhr Valley in World War II. The RAF had to fly over these dams and bridges and hope the bomb would skip exactly right to destroy the dams, thus breaching the water supply that fed the Ruhr factories and causing havoc to the German war machine. It was a typical British war movie of the time, a true story. Todd played Guy Gibson, the RAF commander of the operation. I think the film had its premiere in Ottawa. Richard Todd spoke after the premiere. I didn't go to the premiere, but I did see the movie.

Todd was staying in the presidential suite on the sixth floor of the Chateau Laurier Hotel, one of the most prestigious hotels in Ottawa. And it's still there! Geoff and I were determined to get his autograph, so off we went to the hotel, and we waited in front of that suite – four, five, six hours. Late in the afternoon, a gentleman by the name of Gord Atkinson came by. He was an announcer and interviewer for CFRA, a radio station for which I later worked. He had come to do a radio interview with Richard Todd. He asked, "What are you kids doing here?" We replied, "We're hoping to meet Richard Todd and get his autograph." "How long have you been here?" "Most of the day," we responded. He was shocked. "This is outrageous! I'll have a word with the PR man. There's no reason why you shouldn't meet him. I'm going to interview him in twenty minutes." So Gord went into the suite, and a few minutes later he came back out. "I'm sorry, guys. He doesn't have the time. He appreciated your coming and thanks anyway." And that was that.

Years later, while performing at the Chateau Laurier Hotel, I stayed in that very same suite. I kept opening the door all day long, just in case there were a couple of kids out there waiting for my autograph. There never were, but I'm telling you, if there had been, I'd have brought them in and given them hotdogs and hamburgers. It's funny how you remember things like that.

By the way, I've done my version of *A Christmas Carol* six times: twice as a record; once as a television special, where I played all the parts; once as a live radio show; a stage version; and then on *The Ed Sullivan Show* when I told the entire story in three minutes. I don't know how I pulled off that last one! It was so short; I'm not even sure Scrooge was in it! But I always thought *A Christmas Carol* was the perfect vehicle for me because I could cast anybody, any one of my impressions, in the various roles.

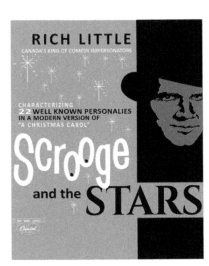

My second album

My very first attempt at *A Christmas Carol* was when I was eighteen. I decided I would make a record of it in my house, and then sell it to a record company. I thought Jack Benny would make the perfect Scrooge. I've since changed my mind – I now prefer W.C. Fields. Benny is cheap, which is perfect when you're playing a miser, but his image, on the whole, is too loveable. Fields, on the other hand, is perfect because he hated children, drank like a fish, and was a cantankerous old man, not much loved in real life.

So I bought a fifty-dollar tape recorder and taped *Scrooge and the Stars* in my bedroom, with bed sheets hanging around the walls to get better sound. I had no idea what to do with it when it was done, but some years later I recorded another album called *My Fellow Canadians* – a spoof on the then Prime Minister of Canada, John Diefenbaker. This somehow became the biggest comedy album in Canadian history. The management at Capitol Records was so pleased with this new album that they agreed to put out *Scrooge and the Stars*. There was only one problem. I had no idea what condition the tape was in. There were more than five hundred edits, all of them done with Scotch tape!

The Spirit of Christmas Present was "played" by John F. Kennedy. Just as the record was about to be pressed, Kennedy was assassinated. For obvious reasons, Capitol thought it would be in bad taste to release it, particularly because the Spirit of Christmas Present had this line: "Scrooge, my life upon this earth is brief: as a matter of fact, it ends tonight." So, I quickly got out some more Scotch tape and recast the Spirit of Christmas Present with Lloyd Bridges of *Sea Hunt*. A few copies of the Kennedy version had been pressed, however. I don't have one, but I've heard there are a few still floating around somewhere and they've become something of a collector's item.

Here I was, at the age of 25, with a major record company picking up this primitive recording, promoting it, and actually selling it. It was a big thrill for me. This was surely my first big step into the world of show business.

So after all this, how did I actually become an impersonator? Well, by accident really.

I wanted to be an actor from the day I saw my first movie. Like most kids, I was bored at school. I used to watch my teachers, and I noticed the way they walked and talked. I picked up on their expressions and their little idiosyncrasies. I was less interested in what they said, than how they said it. Obviously, I wasn't the greatest student in the world, because I was observing rather than listening. Before long I was imitating my teachers: at first, not the voice, just the mannerisms. I'd get up in front of the class first thing in the morning, before the teacher arrived, and I'd do an imitation. It was mostly physical, although I might do a couple of their particular sayings. The kids ate it up. We'd have a lookout at the door. When the lookout signaled that the teacher was coming, I'd rush back to my seat, and we'd all sit up straight at our desks. Then, the teacher would walk into the classroom and do exactly what I'd just been doing. He or she would open a book the way I'd just done it, sit down the way I'd just sat down, and use an expression I'd just used. The kids would just scream with laughter, and the poor teacher had no idea what was going on. How could "Good morning boys and girls" be so funny? The teachers must have thought they were very amusing because the kids laughed at everything they said and everything they did. Only the kids knew that they had seen it all once before that same morning.

Yours truly at age 18

When I saw how popular this was, I began to study all my teachers. And it wasn't long before I was able to imitate their voices as well as their gestures and mannerisms, including the women. I really had the principal's voice down pat. Clarence Bell, the principal, reminded me of W.C. Fields. He had a bulbous nose and a lisp, and I could do him perfectly. No surprise that I became very popular at school, at school concerts and Saturday night dances, where I would get up and "do" the teachers. I think they were all a little bit afraid of me. After all, it was one thing to imitate them; but to ask me a question in class and hear me answer it (usually incorrectly) in their own voice? That was surely what they didn't want to hear!

I realized very early that imitating was a way to get attention, so I started adding other people to my repertoire, such as local politicians. I could imitate Ottawa's mayor, Charlotte Whitton, perfectly. She was a bit like Tugboat Annie, with a kind of raspy voice. I could also imitate our Prime Minister, and many of my friends. I even did an impression of my father. It wasn't very good, but I got a kick out of the way my father would just stare at me and wonder why I was talking in this strange voice.

Even though I had the ability to imitate, by the time I was fifteen my real interest was in the theater. I talked about nothing but actors and acting. One lazy summer, my mother decided to take me down to the Ottawa Little Theater to study acting "as a hobby." I ended up performing several

Learning voices

teenage roles in amateur plays. I learned quite a bit from a fellow by the name of Bill Glen. He was a little older than I was, and he gave me drama lessons on weekends. We got on well, and he really helped me.

My main interest was, and always has been, drama. I know I'm an impersonator; therefore, I must be a comedian. But I never really set out to be a comedian. I didn't know impersonators had to be funny. I'd just imitate someone, the audience would recognize who it was, and they'd applaud. Then I'd do another and they'd recognize it and applaud some more. I'd do this for a few minutes and that was my act.

So, it began to dawn on me that *what* I was saying was just as important as *how* I was saying it. I could amuse people with my impressions, but I also had to amuse them with "content." I didn't know there were people such as comedy writers, so I'd get by doing scenes I'd memorized from movies. In the beginning, it was usually a serious scene, so I didn't get many laughs. However, I did get a lot of applause, and that's when I concluded that I had to be funny, too. I started reading joke books and watching comedians, and slowly got an idea of what I should say for each character I was impersonating. I don't think I was terribly funny at the beginning, but then I was such a young kid that people would laugh and applaud at just about anything I said. Gradually, I realized that the material was just as important as the impression. I needed some sort of "hook" – famous stars sneezing, famous stars laughing, famous stars crying, that sort of thing. What did pets of famous stars sound like? (Of course, they sounded like their owners!) I still do those little routines today. I kick around ideas and think, why not famous stars doing Shakespeare? John Wayne as King Lear? Now that's funny! Famous stars who can't sing at all belting out some oldie? Funny.

My friend Geoff Scott and I put together routines and we started entertaining around Ottawa at parties, school dances, local fairs, and so on.

Then we got a little more ambitious and branched out to perform at the Knights of Columbus, the Shriners, B'nai Brith, and other local organizations. We'd do a little 10- to 15-minute routine, with impressions of local politicians and a few movie stars. We weren't great, but we weren't terrible. We were young, and people thought we were kind of cute. We'd completely forgotten about tracing comic books and pasting pictures of stars in scrapbooks. We focused on our new hobby: impersonations. It was strictly a hobby. I never dreamed it would end up being my life's work.

One day, a member of the Knights of Columbus said, "We'd like you kids to come down and entertain at our annual meeting. We'll give you five bucks each." We thought, "Five bucks? Are you kidding? For doing impressions? Money???" So we did it, and we each walked away with five bucks in our pockets. A couple of weeks later, we were asked to entertain at some other charity event, and we made another five or ten dollars. That's when we started to take this whole thing more seriously. Wouldn't you?

We started to get a bit of a reputation in Ottawa. Maybe the general public didn't know who we were yet, but everyone at school sure did. All Canadian television shows were produced in Toronto at that time, and gradually word got around that there were two teen-aged kids in Ottawa who were pretty good impersonators. Well, maybe not pretty good, but certainly enthusiastic!

Me & Geoff Scott off to Toronto: 1955

We were invited to compete in a talent show called *Pick the Stars*. We took a plane to Toronto and auditioned, and were selected as one of the contestants. We were up against four other acts, and were voted number one! We won that week's contest. We went on to the finals at the end of the year, but we lost. I think we came in second. But this made us realize that we could have a career as impersonators. This was when we really started to take it seriously.

Finally, we had hit the big time: Toronto! Not only that, but on television too! It wasn't long before we were doing variety shows there. They

"Bus Stop"

"The Aries" - Phony sideburns, phony mustache, real acting

"Desperate Hours"

weren't very elaborate – no huge sets, cast, or orchestras – just acts done in front of a curtain. The audience sat on wooden chairs, which consisted of about thirty people, although it looked like more on television.

We were "Geoff Scott and Rich Little: Ottawa's most talked-about young talents." I kept working on material, working on the voices, doing impressions. Geoff gradually became more interested in journalism – he wanted to work for a newspaper. I suspect his parents told him, "You'd better think about a real career. These impressions are fine, but you can't make a life's work out of doing them." Well, I may have thought the same thing at the time, but I was determined to do more voices than anyone had ever done before. My technique was very simple: speed.

I had noticed that Frank Gorshin, George Kirby, Larry Storch, and a few other impersonators who came before me would say, "Kirk Douglas," then turn around, fix their hair, get into character then turn back to the audience as Kirk Douglas. My technique was rapid fire: do Kirk Douglas, then Burt Lancaster, then John Wayne, then George Burns – all one after the other without preparing the audience for the changes. They'd be amazed at how fast

I could switch from voice to voice. I don't think anyone had used this technique before.

About the time we turned twenty, Geoff and I broke up as a comedy team. I went on to act at the Ottawa Little Theater in a number of plays such as *The Heiress, Desperate Hours,* and *Bus Stop,* for which I won the Eastern Ontario Drama Festival award as best actor. I told this, years later, to Don Murray, who was in the movie of the same name. He said, "You must have been good in it." I said, "No, I was just imitating you." I divided my time between acting and impressions. I hired a manager. His name was Gib Kerr. He owned a dance studio in Ottawa, and he had absolutely no experience at being a manager. But he believed in me and started to book me as a single all around the Ottawa valley area – little towns such as Arnprior, Smith's Falls, and Pembroke, all wanting to book some kind of entertainment for some organization, fair, or event, and looking for something different.

Then, two great Canadian writers, Peppiatt and Aylesworth, wrote some material for me. In fact, I probably owe my whole career to Peppiatt and Aylesworth. Not only did they write my stage act, but they also got me dates on countless variety shows in Toronto as well as appearances on *The Jimmy Dean Show, The Julie Andrews Show,* and a number of specials. It was they who called Gib Kerr about my appearing on *The Judy Garland Show.* Gib said, "I'm not sure Rich can make that date. He's got an engagement in Arnprior. There's a sheep-shearing contest up there, and they've hired him to do 15 or 20 minutes for twenty dollars. I'm not sure I can get him out of it." "Gib," I said, "I'm out of it."

So, as the New Year of 1964 was rung in, I packed up my things, hopped into my Rambler, and headed for Los Angeles and *The Judy Garland Show.*

Judy Garland

Where It Really All Began

$\mathcal{J}$t was the thrill of my life to appear on Judy Garland's television show. For many years, I remembered *The Judy Garland Show* as being my first American television appearance, but it really wasn't; it was my second. I did *The Jimmy Dean Show* out of New York first, but I hardly remember that appearance. But I have vivid memories of doing *The Judy Garland Show.*

I had met Mel Tormé in Toronto in 1963. He was playing at a local club, and I went backstage to see him. We hit it off immediately. I don't think anyone, with the exception of Robert Osborne, knew more about movies than Mel Tormé. He was intrigued by the fact that I was doing impressions of Dana Andrews, William Holden, Jack Hawkins, Sterling Hayden, Trevor Howard, Michael Rennie, and George Brent. These were not your run-of-the-mill impressions – most guys were doing Edward G. Robinson, James Cagney, and Jimmy Stewart. After rehearsals, we'd go back to the Holiday Inn where he was staying, and sit up until four in the morning while I did my entire repertoire for him. Sometimes he'd put bed-sheets up on the wall of the basement conference room and we'd watch 16-millimeter movies until two or three in the morning. He had a projector and all the equipment. I remember watching *Merrill's Marauders* starring Jeff Chandler (I think that was Jeff's last movie and one of his best), and Mel did a running commentary throughout the whole film.

One day Mel brought a tape recorder to my hotel room and said, "I've written a script for all the voices you do, and I want you to record it for me." I must have recorded thirty or forty impressions on that tape, including James Mason, with whom Judy Garland had worked on *A Star Is Born*. Mel took the tape to Hollywood when he was hired to do *The Judy Garland Show*. Mel wasn't the musical director (that was Mort Lindsey), but he did "special musical material" for the show.

Besides Mel, the two Canadian writers, Peppiatt and Aylesworth, pitched me for *The Judy Garland Show*. They happened to be there when

Me & Mel Tormé – "On Parade" Canadian variety show: 1963

Mel eventually played the tape for Judy. They just kept pitching: "Listen, not only does he do Lloyd Bridges, he also does Fred MacMurray, and Alfred Hitchcock!" Judy said, "Yeah, he's good. But to tell you the truth, impersonators make me fart!" This was a word Mel detested (I think most of us do), and he thought, "I'll never get Rich on this show if that's the way she feels about impersonators."

But, she listened to the tape a bit longer, and then she said, "Oh, that's pretty good!" Finally, when she got to my impression of James Mason in *A Star Is Born*, she really sat up and took notice. "Play that again…" she said. She loved James Mason, and she had gotten along extremely well with him on the set. I'd already met Mason at the Shakespeare Festival in Stratford, Ontario, when I was eighteen years old. I tried to shake his hand, but he pulled away. "No, use this hand," he said. "I cut my little finger on a piece of whalebone while making *20,000 Leagues Under the Sea*, and it's still healing." I said, "Mr. Mason, I loved you in *A Star Is Born.*" He responded, "Unfortunately, my best scenes were left on the cutting room floor." Anyway, Judy loved Mason, and she liked my impression of Mason *a lot*. She paused for a moment, then said, "Book him on the show." So, I have to add James Mason to the list of people to thank for my rise in show business, along with Mel Tormé, Frank Peppiatt, and John Aylesworth.

Judy was like Dean Martin in that neither of them rarely came for rehearsals. I met with her briefly early in the week for a talk-through, and she was very pleasant at that first meeting. She seemed a bit bored while we were discussing what I was going to do on the show. Suddenly, she said, "Rich, do you like movies?" I said, "Movies? I adore movies!" She replied, "We should get out of here and go to a movie. Let's leave these boring people." I exclaimed, "Are you serious?" She said she was. But then she got involved in something else and the hour got late. I often thought that if we had left immediately, I could have gone to the movies with Judy Garland! In a way, I'm glad we didn't go, because across the street from the studio was a theater playing *Ambush at Tomahawk Gap,* a terrible movie.

Me with Judy on
"The Judy Garland Show": 1964

Appearing on *The Judy Garland Show* was an amazing experience for me. I was young, green, and very wide-eyed. I sent my tuxedo to be pressed before the show. Gib took it to a nearby dry cleaning establishment and went by to pick it up at seven o'clock that night. We were taping at eight. About 7:30, I started to get dressed. "Where are the pants?" I inquired. Gib said, "They're with the jacket." "No they aren't!" "They must have slipped off the hanger." "You're kidding me! You mean the pants slipped off the hanger on the way back from the cleaners?" "Well, if they're not here, they must have," Gib concluded. We couldn't find them anywhere. Now I was really panicked. It was about twenty minutes to eight. So Gib went to Gary Smith, the director, and said, "Rich has no pants." Gary laughed and said, "Please, this is no time for jokes."

"No, it's true. He has no trousers. We lost them," Gib explained. We ended up borrowing a pair of pants from one of the ushers. They were a bit short, but the camera never showed the bottom of my legs. That's how I did *The Judy Garland Show* – my jacket, and an usher's pair of pants.

Taping Judy's show was quite interesting. I was slated to appear later in the program, but things just dragged on and on. I remember waiting… and waiting…and waiting. Hours went by. They were having "technical problems." I don't think I did my spot until eleven o'clock or midnight. Of course, when I knew more about Judy Garland, I knew that most of the problems consisted of getting her out of her dressing room. She may have been a little tipsy, or she may have taken too many pills. Or maybe she was just plain scared – it could have been anything. Her dressing room was built like a little home. Just as in *The Wizard of Oz*, it had a yellow brick road leading to it. It was quite cute. For all I know, she'd barricaded herself in there, and they had to keep coaxing her out to do her numbers.

We also had Peter Lawford on the show. He was a bit distant; he had his own problems. He was also drinking quite heavily at the time, so between the two of them, things didn't go over too well. I think we finished taping the show around two in the morning. It was a difficult show. But, when Judy wasn't drinking, and when she was one-on-one, she was an absolute delight with a great sense of humor.

What really made my appearance on Judy's show successful was the fact that we didn't rehearse. She had no idea what I was going to do until we went to tape it in front of an audience. Peppiatt and Aylesworth had come up with the idea of my doing the song "The Man That Got Away" from *A Star Is Born,* but I would "talk" it in various voices as the music played softly behind me. Judy would call out different names, and I'd immediately go into that voice. I did "The Man That Got Away" as Alfred Hitchcock, Fred MacMurray, John Wayne, Jimmy Stewart, Jack Benny – and finished off with James Mason. Each time I did a new voice, she'd be hearing it for the first time. Her reaction was incredible. By the time I got to Mason, she was simply enthralled with what I was doing. If you get a chance to look at that appearance today (it's available on DVD and on YouTube), you won't be able to take your eyes off Judy. It's her reactions, rather than my actual performance that make it so great. She turned out to be the best audience in the world!

My appearance on *The Judy Garland Show* led to many other variety shows. I went on to do Flip Wilson, Glen Campbell, Carol Burnett, *The Hollywood Palace*, Ed Sullivan, Dean Martin – you name it. I must have done at least thirty or forty different variety shows over the next five years, all as a result of that one appearance on *The Judy Garland Show*.

But after my appearance on her show, I never spoke to Judy Garland again. I did see her one more time in England, a year or so before she died. She was in a restaurant with Johnnie Ray, the great singer of the '50s, and a couple of other people. I wanted to go over and say hello, but then I thought she wouldn't remember who I was, so I didn't.

She was the best audience in the world for what I did. For a woman who didn't like impersonators, she sure didn't show it on the screen. And she never farted!

George Burns

My Welcome to Hollywood

I spoke with George Burns even before I had a chance to meet him. The result? One of the funniest put-downs I've ever had in my life. Before I tell you about it, some background is in order.

When I came to the U.S. from Canada to do *The Judy Garland Show*, it was largely through the efforts of my buddy Mel Tormé. When I arrived in Los Angeles, I checked into a hotel near the Farmer's Market on Fairfax Avenue, and then went across the street to meet him in his office at CBS. While we were figuring out what kind of routine I'd do on the show, and kicking around the idea of doing "The Man That Got Away" with various voices, I realized, for some strange reason, that I'd never done George Burns for him. So when I did George, he couldn't get over it. I had to do it for everyone in the office, and they were all agog with the performance.

Me with George Burns doing Jack Benny
on "Hollywood Palace": 1966

Mel asked, "Has George heard this?" I said, "Well, of course not. I've never even been to the States before. How could George have heard my impression of him?" Mel responded, "Well, he's gonna love it! He's got a great sense of humor. And I don't think I've ever heard anyone else do George Burns, so he'll be quite thrilled you're doing him. Why don't we phone him up right now, and you can do it for him? I've got his number right here in my Rolodex. He lives in Beverly Hills somewhere, and you can do it for him over the phone." I stammered, "Well, that's great Mel, but what am I going to say?" "Oh, you'll think of something funny," he said. "I will? For George Burns?" I said aloud. Then I'm thinking to myself, "Gee, I'd better think about this before we do it. George is pretty quick. He's one of the best." But right as I was standing there trying to think of what to say, Mel had already reached George and was handing me the phone.

I was dumbfounded! I just couldn't believe he'd reached George that fast. But I took the phone from Mel, and in George's voice, I said, "George, this is Rich Little. I've just come down from Canada to do *The Judy Garland Show*. I'm an impressionist. As a matter of fact, I do an impression of you, and I thought I'd phone you up and do it for you." Without missing a beat, George said, "Gee, that's great kid. I'd love to hear it sometime." And hung up!

Everyone in the room listening on the speaker got the biggest kick out of this. I'd done my imitation of George Burns for George Burns, and he pretended he didn't know what I was doing! I eventually learned this was typical of George. Years later, when I got to know him pretty well, we were sitting around chatting one day, and I said, "Do you remember one day back in the '60s when Mel Tormé put me up to doing you on the phone, and you said, 'I'd love to hear it sometime' and hung up?" George replied, "Yeah, I knew it wasn't me, because I was on the other end of the phone."

George Burns & me on "Hollywood Palace" doing an appendix routine

The first time I actually met George was on *The Hollywood Palace*, where we did a little routine. By this time, I'd done quite a few variety shows, so he was aware of me and my impression of him. The two of us came out and I said to George (as George), "Well, George, how's your brother Willie?" "My brother Willie's all right now after the operation," he said. "After the operation? What operation?" "Well, he had appendicitis, and he has a scar on his neck." "Wait a minute," I responded. "Isn't the appendix down here in the abdomen?" "Well, yeah, but he was so ticklish they had to operate up here on his neck." Actually, this was part of an old routine George did with Gracie Allen, only George played Gracie's part and I played George's.

Down through the years, we would often end up on one show or another together, or we'd meet in airports, or sometimes I'd go by his office and we'd just talk. He loved to talk. He loved to reminisce. He didn't talk about history — he *was* history. He loved to talk about the early days of vaudeville, about Al Jolson, Georgie Jessel, Sophie Tucker, and so many others. I couldn't help thinking at the time that there was probably nobody left in show business with his kind of knowledge, because nobody had lived this long. I always wished I had a tape recorder on hand when he was telling these stories, because this was fascinating information. He went all the way back to Buster Keaton, Harold Lloyd, Fanny Brice — people like that. And, he had total recall. He could recall bits of dialogue as if he'd heard them yesterday. He had an incredible mind.

George Burns was a tease. You never really knew if he was putting you on or not. He could be telling you a story about his career or perhaps about someone he'd known in the past, and you'd be spellbound listening to him. And then, as he got near the end of the story, he'd suddenly say, "No, that's not true. I made that all up. It never happened. Now let me tell you the true story…" And he'd start all over again! This time the story would be even funnier, but you still couldn't be sure if the story was true or not.

Me, Phyllis McGuire & my daughter Bria with George Burns at his 95th birthday celebration

The last time I saw George was at Caesars Palace in Las Vegas. I was with my daughter, Bria, who absolutely adored him. Younger people loved him. I think they admired that he was as bright and as hip as he was given his age. I'd sit and listen to him for hours, which was the best thing you could do with George Burns. If you tried to top him, he'd just top you back. He was too smart, too quick, and had been at it too long for you to think you could outwit him. He was a remarkable man, and I believe he had one of the great comedy minds of all time. Even though his body gave out at 100, his mind never did.

Jack Benny

The Greatest of Them All

*J*ack Benny was a love – he really was. He didn't have much of an ego; he was very easygoing, and he loved to laugh, especially at other comedians. He took an interest in me from the very beginning of my career. I first met Jack on Steve Allen's talk show in 1964. Everyone knew I did Jack Benny, so Steve asked me if I would do him on the show. Unbeknownst to me, Jack was in the audience. When I started my routine, a voice from the back of the theater yelled out, "You're doing it all wrong! You're doing it all wrong!" Of course, the audience reacted with thunderous applause. Jack came up on stage, and for the next five minutes proceeded to tell me how I could make my impression of him better. When I put my hand up to my face, I'd used four fingers. He only used three. He said, "Rich, you'll get a better laugh with three fingers, because everybody knows that three is a funnier number than four." Of course, I believed all of this – I was pretty gullible back in those days – so it was hard to tell if Jack was putting you on or not, just like George Burns. Then he said that my "Well!" was all wrong, that I was hitting it too hard, that I was saying, "WELL!" when I should really be very quiet – a softer "Well." He said, "This will really improve the impression. And," he added, "the walk needs work too. You're walking like Bob Hope." It was a very funny show.

Jack Benny & me on "The Steve Allen Show": 1964

I idolized Jack Benny, and I think he liked me, too. He'd go out of his way to see my show wherever I was appearing. He'd always come to see me when I was appearing at The Palmer House in Chicago. He always preferred to sit in the audience and watch the show – he never watched backstage. He loved my George Burns, but he really got a big kick out of my politicians. When I did Richard Nixon, he'd just pound the table and laugh. His favorite impression was Spiro Agnew, Richard Nixon's vice president, which kind of surprised me. I guess this was because, as I later found out, Spiro was a friend of his. I didn't even know they knew one another, and no one else did an impression of Spiro Agnew. He thought it was my best impression. So, whenever we'd appear on a television show together, he'd ask me to do Spiro Agnew. He said that when Agnew told him he was going to resign as vice president, Jack told him, "Rich Little does you better than you do. You resign, and Rich Little can take over as you." Agnew didn't even have a clue who I was!

Jack also liked my Johnny Carson. He was very fond of Johnny, who was sort of a protégé of his, and the admiration was mutual. I think Jack's influence on Johnny was evident – the deadpan look, the looking away and looking around that Johnny did were pretty much the same as Jack's demeanor. And their timing was very, very similar. One of Johnny's favorite stories involved Jack, and he used to tell it over and over again on his show. After a while, he had told it so many times that everyone would say, "Oh no! He's not going to tell that Jack Benny story again!" I'm not quite sure how true that is, but it sounds true to me. Here's how it went:

Me doing Carson on "The Tonight Show" with Johnny Carson

Jack wanted to plug one of his NBC specials, so he called Johnny at home one night hinting that he'd like to come on the show the following week. Johnny kind of brushed him off, "Oh yeah, sure Jack, sure, sure." He didn't give him a definitive answer. In fact, he was actually a bit cool towards him. When he hung up, Jack was a little upset by Johnny's indifference, and told his manager, Irving Fein, about it. So Irving called Johnny and told him that Jack was a little disappointed that Johnny gave him the brush-off. Carson said, "What are you talking about? No, no, no – that was Rich Little doing Jack Benny. I can tell an impression from the real person. It was Rich Little." "No, Johnny, it was the real Jack Benny," insisted Irving. "You're kidding!" exclaimed Johnny. "Believe me," said Irving, "it was Jack." Finally, Johnny was convinced and he called Jack back, terribly apologetic. "I really thought you were Rich Little," he said. Of course you can come on the show next week!" "Fine," replied Jack. "Just don't send the check to Rich Little!" Now *that* was Jack Benny.

Jack Benny & me – both doing Benny

One time, I was doing a couple of weeks at The Palmer House in Chicago. On the afternoon of our opening night when I was rehearsing for the show, one of the stagehands came in and said, "Jack Benny's upstairs in the second floor ballroom rehearsing for a private party for some organization." "Well, that's great," I said. "I haven't seen Jack for a while. I'll go up and see him." I walked into the ballroom and asked someone where Jack was, and was told, "He's around here somewhere." I started looking all over for him, but I couldn't find him. Then I heard a violin, and I thought "That's gotta be Jack." I kept pushing open various doors, trying to find him. As I got closer to the washroom, the sound of the violin grew louder. I walked in and pushed open the door to the second stall. There was Jack, sitting on the toilet, playing his violin. "Rich, I'm glad you dropped by," he said. "I heard you were opening downstairs, and I was going to look you up." "Jack, what are you doing?" I asked. "Well, I'm rehearsing." "In a toilet?" "Well, I'm kind of used to it. You see at home, my wife, Mary can't stand my violin playing, so I usually end up playing in the bathroom where she can't hear me. It's a friendly environment." He looked around. "Is there anybody else in here?" "I don't know," I replied honestly. "Well, check, will you?" he asked. I noticed that one other stall was locked. "I think there's another guy in the stall next to you," I whispered. "Well, see if he's standing?" came Jack's reply. "Standing?" "Yes. See if I got a standing ovation?" *That* was Jack Benny.

```
HDA227(1558) (2-08093E018)PD  01/18/73  1558
ICS IMPMRNCZ CSP
ZCZC 2134647618 TDRN HOLLYWOOD CA 38 01-18 0358P EST
PMS RICH LITTLE, DLR, DLR
7250 FRANKLIN AVE NUMBER 907
HOLLYWOOD CA 90046
SAW YOU LAST NIGHT JUST GREAT BUT YOU HAVE GOT ME SO CONFUSED
I DONT KNOW WHETHER IM JACK BENNY OR WHETHER YOURE JACK BENNY
I DONT KNOW WHETHER YOURE ME OR IM YOU, ANYWAY THANKS YOUR FRIEND
RICH
```

I once did a sketch on television with Phyllis Diller, in which I played Jack. It was very funny and very well written, and I had a lot of fun doing it. A couple of days after it aired, I got the following telegram from Jack: "Dear Rich: I caught you the other night on television doing me, and I was really impressed. In fact, you were so good, I don't know who the hell I am! I don't know whether I'm you, you're me, we're both me, or we're both you. Anyway, I thought it was just terrific." He signed it "Rich." *That* was Jack Benny.

I can still see Jack playing the quarter slot machines at the Sands Hotel in Las Vegas in the wee hours of the morning. One night after I'd finished my show at midnight, I saw him sitting at a slot machine as I was on my way to the coffee shop for breakfast. On the way back to my room, around 2:30, he was still playing the same machine. I walked over to him and said, "Jack, it's 2:30 in the morning! How long are you going to play this machine?" "Until my string breaks." *That* was Jack Benny.

One time, we did *The Tonight Show* together. Because of the three-hour time difference between the East and West coasts, the show was taped at six o'clock for its 11:30 p.m. airtime. After the show, I was hanging out in Jack's dressing room, and I asked him, "Are you going straight home or do you want to get something to eat?" "Well, I'd like a cup of soup. They've got the greatest chicken soup right here in the NBC commissary. I mean, I've never tasted soup as good as this," he replied. I asked, "From the commissary?" The NBC commissary was, to say the least, not noted for the quality of its food. "Yeah. You've never tasted it?" "I don't think so," I replied. "Well, you gotta try this soup. I've been thinking about this for weeks. As a matter of fact, the only reason I agreed to do the show tonight is because of the chicken soup. Let's go down to the commissary." "Ok, I'll join you," I conceded. So Jack, Irving, and a small group of us headed down a long hallway to the NBC commissary for a cup of extra-special chicken soup. We walked, and we walked, and we walked some more. Finally, we got to the commissary – and it was closed! Jack tried the door, and said, "I can't believe it! They're closed!" "Yeah, I guess it's a little late," I said. "They can't be closed!" he insisted. "I only took the show because of the soup!" "Well, sorry Jack, but it's definitely closed," I added. Irving was tapping on the glass, hoping someone was in there, but the place was dead. Now Jack was really upset. He said, "I had my heart set on a cup of NBC's chicken soup. I've been thinking about it for weeks, and now they're closed. They can't do this to me!" "We should have gotten the soup earlier," I said. He replied, "They *never* closed this early. Irving, keep banging on the glass. Is there any way we can force the door open?" Everyone yelled, "No, we can't do that Jack. C'mon, it's not that important." "Well it is to me! See if there's another way in there." Collectively, we all tried other doors, looking for another way in. But there wasn't any. The place was locked up tighter than a fortress. "I guess that's it Jack," I said. "No it isn't. No it isn't! I'm not giving up!" he hollered. "Well, even if we get in, how are we going to get the soup? Everything's probably put away." He said, "We don't know that!" Meanwhile, Irving kept banging on the glass.

At long last, a lady came to the door. I don't know if she was a cleaning lady or what she was doing there, but she unlocked the door.

Jack gasped, "Thank heaven you're here!" "What's wrong?" she asked. Jack begged, "I've gotta have a cup of chicken soup!" "Well, everything's put away," she insisted. "It must be here!" exclaimed Jack. So we started rummaging through the kitchen, found the refrigerators, opened them up, and sure enough, Jack found the soup! The woman was nice enough to heat it up for us, and Jack was in his element. This was the greatest thing that had ever happened to him! Against all odds, he had gotten his chicken soup. Personally, I thought it was just average soup, but Jack couldn't stop raving about it. In fact, by this time, he was dancing around like a 25-year-old kid. We started back down the long hallway with extra cups of chicken soup in hand, Jack still raving about it all the way. As we passed by another studio, we could hear music and audience reaction from inside. We stopped and talked with an NBC page, "What's going on in there?" He said, "Lucille Ball's filming her television show." "Really, she's in there right now?" Jack asked. The page said, "Yeah. I think she's

Lucille Ball & me on an episode of "Here's Lucy": 1971

in the middle of shooting a sketch," the page answered. Jack turned to Irving. "How much extra soup do we have?" Irving said, "About six cups. Why?" "Let's give some to Lucille Ball. She'll be delighted!" The now slightly-worried page said, "But they're in the middle of taping right now, Mr. Benny. Can you wait until the red light goes off?" Jack responded, "No, the soup will get cold." He opened the door and marched in. We followed meekly behind as Jack walked right on stage, in the middle of a sketch she was doing in front of a live audience! He called out, "Oh Lucy, Lucy…It's Jack Benny!" And of course, the audience went wild. Lucille Ball was quite a trouper and a very smart lady. She realized that if whatever happened next wasn't half-bad, she'd keep it in the show. It was a completely unrehearsed moment, and could be better than anything in the script. As the applause died down, Jack said, "Lucy, I brought you a cup of chicken soup from the commissary. The best chicken soup ever made in the United States." "Jack, that's very sweet of you, but I don't like soup," Lucy responded. "You don't like soup? Have you ever tasted the soup made here?" Jack asked. "No, not really. I just don't care much for soup." Jack pressed on, "I'm crushed… I can't … Won't you try just a little bit of it?" So Lucy took a little sip of the soup. "Hmmm. Not bad," she pronounced. "Not bad? Are you kidding? This is great!" Jack started giving everyone in the cast a sample of the soup. Everyone was taking little sips, some trying to be polite with, "Oh yeah, that's terrific," or "That's the best soup I ever tasted." Then Jack took the cup and walked out among the audience, getting them to take a sip of the soup. Of course they were just delighted to be part of all this. The cameras captured the whole thing; with Jack handing out soup to the audience telling them they'd never had such great soup in their lives. He finally went back on stage and left the audience in stitches. Then Lucille Ball said, "Jack Benny, ladies and gentlemen." And they applauded again. Jack cried, "Never mind me, let's hear it for the soup!" The audience went along with this and gave the soup a standing ovation. As we walked out, he turned to me and said, "See? I told you it was the greatest soup ever made." *That* was jack Benny.

When we got back out into the hallway, I said, "Well, I guess we'd better get going." But Jack said, "No, let's go back and get some more soup. The audience ate it all." At this point, Irving piped up, "Geez, Jack. It's ten o'clock. We can't go back and get that lady to go through all of that again!" "But now we don't have any extra for tomorrow," Jack lamented. "Well, we'll just have to come back and do another *Tonight Show* so I can get some more of this great soup." *That* was Jack Benny.

Another time when we were backstage at The Palmer House, Jack asked me, "Rich, how do you like The Palmer House?" "It's a good place to perform, good orchestra, nice people…" I said. But he said, "No, not just the room, the whole hotel." "Well, the hotel is very nice too," I added. "Nice?" he said. "They've got the fluffiest towels here of any hotel in America. I've seen hotel towels all over the world. I've felt them, I've measured them, I've wrapped myself in them and I've dried myself with them. And, I'm here to tell you The Palmer House towels are the fluffiest, that's why this is one of my favorite places to perform. I always make a point of doing one or two shows a year here, because you'll never find towels like this anywhere else. They're so big and fluffy; I can hardly fit them in my suitcase." *That* was Jack Benny.

Jack would sometimes say things such as, "I don't like Chicago. The water isn't as good as it is in New York," or "The sheets on the bed are the best sheets of any hotel I've ever been in." George Burns once told a story where Jack had just signed the greatest deal with NBC for the new season. They'd given him more money than they'd given almost any other performer, plus he got a percentage. After signing the deal in his agent's office, George said Jack rushed back to his house. Everyone thought he was going to tell Mary about the great deal he'd just signed. He was so excited, he couldn't wait to tell her the good news... That if you travel at 23 miles an hour down Sunset Boulevard, you'd only hit one red light! This was much more exciting news than the fact that he'd just signed one of the biggest deals in show business! *That* was Jack Benny.

You'd be sitting in a restaurant with him, and he'd say to the waiter, "I'd like some toast, marmalade and two small, very tiny, poached eggs." "Fine, Mr. Benny. Coming up," the waiter responded. "They've got to be really small," Jack emphasized. "Well, sir, what do you mean by that?" the waiter asked. "I don't want those great big eggs. Do you have any little eggs?" Apparently, this made a real difference to Jack. The waiter said, "I'll check Mr. Benny." Being curious, I asked, "Where would you get tiny eggs?" "Well, from a tiny chicken. Where else?" Then Jack would say to the waiter, "If you can't find any tiny eggs, I'll just have the toast and marmalade." I don't remember if the waiter found any tiny eggs, but if he had, Jack would have told everybody that the tiny eggs in that coffee shop were the best that he had ever tasted. *That* was Jack Benny.

Jack also loved to walk. Sometimes he'd take a walk late at night, after a show, during which he'd talk about his career and tell you great stories. He'd always put on a trench coat, tie the belt in a knot, and wear a snap-brimmed hat. He tried to look like Humphrey Bogart. He'd put the collar up – the whole bit – and off we'd go. As we walked along the street one night, I said, "It's amazing that people don't recognize you." "No, they think I'm Humphrey Bogart," he responded. One time we were walking through a park at about 11:30 at night, and some fellow *did* recognize him, and asked him for an autograph. Jack put on his Humphrey Bogart lisp, and said, "Sure, sweetheart. What's your name?" Of course, he signed it as Jack Benny. After the guy left, Jack said, "He's going to be disappointed after he takes a look at that piece of paper. I'm sure he thought I was Bogie." *That* was Jack Benny.

I don't think I ever enjoyed being with two people as much as I enjoyed being with Jack Benny and George Burns. One of the reasons may have been that my father absolutely adored both of them. He thought *The Jack Benny Show* and *The Burns and Allen Show* were terrific. I'm not sure whether I had started imitating them prior to my father's death in 1959 or not, but I've often thought how proud he would have been if he'd known I was chumming around with those two. My dad was never really terribly impressed by celebrities. He was a loner, didn't socialize a great deal, and didn't show his emotions much. But when he liked something, he went all out. And he loved Jack Benny and George Burns.

Jack was very finicky – little things used to please him or disturb him, and George Burns would feed off it and kid him about it. George had no mercy, believing, "Anything for a laugh." Jack could make George smile, and George appreciated Jack's humor, but George wouldn't fall down on the floor, screaming with laughter, the way Jack literally did. George was one of the few people who could break him up, and Jack knew it. He'd say to me, "I'm not going to fall for George. I know what he's going to do to me. He's going to do something outrageous, but I'm not going to fall for it, and I will *not* laugh. I don't care what he does. He can come in with his pants down and a lampshade on his head, but I will *not* laugh." But of course, George would *not* come in with his pants down and a lampshade on his head. He'd come in doing something so funny that Jack would inevitably be on the floor, screaming.

Some of the things George would do to break up Jack were well known, such as the night they were at a dinner party and there was no (and I mean *no*) conversation at all. Everyone was sitting around the table politely eating. Jack finally got up and went over to the mantle, took a cigarette out of the case, and put it in his mouth. George said, "Hold it! Hold it everybody! Everybody quiet, hold it, hold it down! Quiet!" This had very little effect because nobody was talking anyway. George then announced, "Jack's now going to do his famous match trick. Watch this! He's been working on it all week." Of course, Jack had no idea what he was talking about, and had nothing prepared. He just looked kind of embarrassed, lit the cigarette and took a puff. George said, "Oh! A new finish!" and Jack fell to his knees with laughter.

Another time, Jack found out that George was about to check into the same hotel where he was staying. He got George's key in advance, and asked the desk clerk to let him know when George had checked in. He then went up to George's room. The clerk called him sometime later and said, "He's here. He's on his way up." Jack, still in the room, had taken off all his clothes, put a lampshade on his head, put on some white gloves, grabbed a cane, and put spats on his bare feet. He was totally naked and stood on the bed posing, waiting for George. I don't know if George had been tipped off, or if he suspected something, but there was a rattle at the door, and Jack yelled, "Come in!" Rather than George, in walked a maid, who stood aghast, staring at a naked Jack Benny on the bed. Jack said, "No, no! Please no! I'm waiting for George Burns!" And *that* was Jack Benny.

Cary Grant

A Class Act

$\mathcal{S}$everal years ago, the American Film Institute and Entertainment Weekly magazine voted Humphrey Bogart as the greatest movie star of all time. I think he was definitely in the top 20, but certainly not number one. He made five or six great movies: *Casablanca*, of course; *The Caine Mutiny, The Maltese Falcon, The Treasure of the Sierra Madre,* along with others that were pretty entertaining. He also made a few bad pictures, as all big stars have done at some point in their careers. I think there's a distinction, however, between the greatest *movie star* of all time, and the greatest *actor* of all time. If I were to choose the greatest actor of all time, I'd have to nominate Laurence Olivier, because of his immense versatility. His greatest triumphs were on the stage, but he made many great movies, and he took on a variety of roles. Like Bogart, he made a few truly ghastly movies, although most of Olivier's stinkers came at the end of his career. Many people consider Marlon Brando to have been the greatest, especially in terms of his ability to combine the persona of actor and movie star. But I personally felt he was overrated. He popularized a whole new style of acting, the so-called Method Style. The Method Style was considered somehow more "real" than what had come before. He had made several good movies: *A Streetcar Named Desire, On the Waterfront, Viva Zapata* and *The Men* among them, but he also made some of the worst movies ever. In fact, he is a solid contender for the title of "The Star Who Intentionally Made the Most Really Bad Movies." A few notables: *Burn, The Island of Dr. Moreau, The Nightcomers,* and *Reflections in a Golden Eye.*

When it comes down to selecting the most *popular* movie star of all time, I personally would choose either Jimmy Stewart or Cary Grant. In my opinion, Jimmy was a bit more versatile on screen than Cary. Even though Jimmy was usually Jimmy, he did stray from his image from time to time in films such as *The Flight of the Phoenix* and *Fool's Parade.* He could perform drama, he could do light comedy, and he could play a cowboy quite convincingly. Cary Grant, on the other hand, was superb at light comedy. He was the epitome of the suave, sophisticated, debonair type, but not particularly versatile. He never looked too comfortable in a costume movie, and I think he made a conscious decision early in his career to stick to what he did best. He really was an actor who appeared to never make a wrong move. Everything about him projected perfection – his looks, his timing, his reactions. It was an absolutely extraordinary experience to watch him act. Stewart Granger once told me that Cary Grant invented Cary Grant. Granger knew him quite well in the early days, and told me that he came from a rather poor family in Bristol, England. The Cary Grant the public knew was a character that Cary created for himself. The real Cary Grant was a very simple man who liked very simple things; who giggled and laughed a lot, didn't drink champagne all the time, and wasn't really that sophisticated in real life. I certainly agree with what Granger said, because on one occasion we were talking about Alfred Hitchcock, and Cary said to me, "Probably my favorite of all Cary Grant movies is *North by Northwest*. It was the most demanding, the most physical of any picture he ever made with Grant." I thought it was interesting that he said, "…my favorite of all Cary Grant movies…" and not "…the favorite of all my movies was…." It was weird that he talked about himself professionally in the third person. There was a lot of truth in what Granger said.

Meeting Cary Grant in person might have thrown you a bit, because of course, everyone thought of him as he appeared in the movies – someone who was sure of himself and almost a world unto himself. However, the real-life Cary Grant was entirely different. He was a very happy man, full of enthusiasm, who enjoyed life tremendously and wanted everyone else to enjoy it as much as he did. When he "giggled" – which he often did – you'd think, "No, no, Cary Grant wouldn't giggle like that!" But indeed he did. He loved people – especially comedians – and was curious about a host of things.

I met him for the first time when I was performing at the Sands Hotel in Las Vegas. Of course, I'd been imitating him for years on television. I had just finished doing the casino show. No one told me ahead of time that he was in the audience. Probably a good thing. If I had known,

I would have been done in with nervousness! After the show, my then-wife, Jeanne, and her sister dropped by my dressing room to say hello and to tell me they'd be in the coffee shop when I was ready to join them. As they were walking down the empty backstage passageway to the casino, Cary passed them on his way to my dressing room. Needless to say, their eyes grew as big as saucers, and they immediately did an about-face back to the dressing room. Cary came in and introduced himself – as if he needed to! He was still giggling. He just couldn't get over the show. And I'll always remember what he said: "What you do out on that stage for an hour and a half! You make people forget their troubles and you bring back all those wonderful memories. Those great stars, those great movies! Laughter is the best medicine for anybody, and I can't tell you how much all of us in the audience enjoyed not only your performance, but your material, your timing, and of course, your dead-on impressions. I'm a big, big, big fan." My mouth opened but nothing came out. Can you imagine having one of the people you've most admired being someone who admired *you*? When I could find my voice, I was full of questions, so I started to ask him about his movies. "No, no, no, no!" he said. "We don't want to talk about *me*! We want to talk about *you*!"

He really didn't want to talk about his movies. He never did. He was so much more interested in what he felt were "real" things – geography, nature, history, things like that. He took great pride in what he did, because he was a perfectionist; but I think he always felt being a movie star was highly overrated. Nevertheless, whenever he'd say, "Let's not talk about movies," I'd switch to something else. But within three or four minutes later, we'd be back talking about movies again. Then he'd catch himself and start all over again, "No, no, no! I don't want to talk about movies." So we'd change the subject once more, but sure enough, before long, we'd be back talking about movies *again*. He didn't mind talking about *other* people, *other* actors, *other* films. He just didn't want to talk about himself. He was very unassuming. On a good day, I could get him to answer several questions, and talk about certain films. For example, I told him how much I liked *People Will Talk*, a movie he'd made with Jeanne Crain. He told me the only reason he took the picture was so that he could conduct the orchestra in the film. He didn't even read the script! I think one of his best performances was in *None but the Lonely Heart*, with Ethel Barrymore. He told me he put a lot of work into that role and took the film very seriously, even though it bombed at the box office. It proved to be one of the last times he stepped out of the "Cary Grant" mold he had so carefully created for himself. I liked the Cary Grant I spent so much time talking to. I liked the movie Cary Grant too. It was like being a fan of two different people. He was always very good natured with me, and I noticed that he was always friendly towards other people too. I also enjoyed his insatiable curiosity. Someone once told me he charged twenty-five cents for an autograph, and I thought that was a little strange. But then I heard he gave this money to charity, which made absolute sense, knowing the kind of man he was. I understand a lot of celebrities do this nowadays, so Cary Grant was just ahead of the times.

Cary almost always came to see my show when he was in Las Vegas. He'd come backstage, and we'd chat for twenty or thirty minutes. He got a big kick out of it. He always wanted to know when I'd be performing in Vegas, and he'd either say, "I'll be there!" or "Darn, I have to go on a tour for Faberge and I can't make it." He'd often mail me notes: "When will you be performing in Vegas again?" or "I saw you on *Evening at the Pops* doing *Peter and the Wolf* – I think I should have played the duck!" or "I saw you on such-and-such a show" or "I hear you're going to do this or that." He'd always compliment me on a performance and he was always inquisitive as to what I was up to. And, he handwrote each of those little notes himself. Imagine my surprise when one of them said that because of me, he had almost been committed! He was on an airplane listening to an old recording of mine in which I did movie stars singing. When he got to my impression of Jimmy Stewart singing "People," he just cracked up. "I just absolutely lost it," he wrote. "I was in hysterics listening to 'Jimmy' try and sing. I know him so well, and I've heard him try to sing, and it's pretty awful. But when I heard you do it, I was just about in the aisle screaming with laughter. I was afraid the stewardess would call ahead and have me taken to the nearest hospital when the plane landed!" He wanted to know where he could get a copy of that CD. Naturally, I sent it to him.

If Cary hadn't seen my act for a while, he'd ask, "Are you still doing me?" I'd say, "Of course." And he'd ask, "Really? Do they remember me?" And I'd say, "Are you kidding? They'll always remember you." "But I haven't made a picture in years," he'd respond. "Cary, you don't have to have made a picture in years – or for that matter, ever again. The movies you made will be remembered forever." Then he'd retort, "Well, a lot of them were in black and white." And I'd say, "So what? You made so many wonderful movies; they'll be watched for centuries to come." "You really think so?" He was very insecure. I don't think he had an ounce of ego in him. He always wanted to know how I was portraying him in my act and what the latest "bit" was. When I told him, he'd just sit there like a big kid and ask, "Does it get a big laugh? Does it get a bigger laugh, say, than Jimmy Stewart or John Wayne?"

One day we were at a party, and I told him a joke that I was doing as him in my act. Here's how it went: "The other day I was going through my attic, and I found some old clothes that I hadn't worn in years. I actually found the suit that I'd worn in *North by Northwest!* Remember that dark suit I wore throughout the whole film? I picked it up and was going through the pockets when I found a laundry ticket. I said to myself, 'I wonder...no, no, no – that laundry's probably been torn down a long time ago.' But just on a whim, I drove by that address and sure enough, it was still there – after 30 years! I couldn't believe it. So I walked in and put the ticket down on the counter. The girl looked at it and said, 'Ah, yes. Your things will be ready on Friday.'" Well, Cary just screamed at that. Everyone in the room turned to look at him. Still laughing, he took a pen and a slip of paper and wrote the whole thing down. I don't know what he did with it, but I'm sure he told people that joke over and over.

For a time, I lived in Malibu, California. One day, I was having dinner at a local restaurant with my then-wife, Jeanne, and my mother. Cary Grant, his wife Barbara, and some friends were in the next booth. I whispered to my mother, "Cary Grant is in the next booth." She darn near fainted. She could hardly eat. Cary had this effect on everyone – he was one of the very few Hollywood stars who could literally stop traffic. When he entered a room, whether you could see him or not, you knew someone important had just walked in. He had incredible magnetism. Anyway, Cary and his party were studying their menus, and the waiter came over and asked them what they'd like to order. Cary just couldn't decide. Of course, we could hear the whole conversation because we were in the next booth. Then, I heard Cary say to the waiter, "Rich Little does a great Cary Grant. Ask him what I want." So, when the waiter turned to me, in Cary's voice, I ordered Dover sole, scalloped potatoes, and spinach. Then I heard Cary say to the waiter, "I don't want that." So I turned around to him and said, in his voice, "Well, make up your mind what I'm going to eat." "I'll order what you want," he said to me. He then turned to the waiter, and said, "Bring a porterhouse steak, baked potato, and string beans." The waiter brought the two orders, and then we switched them.

When Frank Sinatra celebrated his 70th birthday, Caesars Palace threw him a big televised party, Vegas style. The room was packed with celebrities, and many of Frank's friends and acquaintances were there to entertain: Ernie Borgnine, Robert Merrill, Charlie Callas, and myself among them. I had worked out a little routine constructed around his movies, imitating several of the people who'd worked with him in films. But then I saw Cary sitting right at the edge of the stage, so I made a split-second decision to change course and try a variation on a bit that I'd used when I paid tribute to Jimmy Stewart at one of *The Dean Martin Celebrity Roasts*.

Cary Grant, Barbara & Frank Sinatra, Dean Martin & me at Frank's 70th birthday celebration

I wasn't totally sure where I was going with this, but I walked over to Cary, who was probably scared to death when he saw me approaching. I asked, "Are you Cary Grant? I don't believe it. Say something as Cary Grant." Cary replied, "What do you want me to say?" And to that I responded, "Well, that was pretty good. Now give us your Burt Lancaster." It was a very funny moment, and it got a huge response from the crowd. Cary chuckled throughout the whole thing. It was very heartwarming, largely because, in spite of his discomfort at being caught off guard, he was such a total pro that he had no problem reacting just as "Cary Grant" would be expected to.

He once asked me why I and so many other impersonators did this "Judy, Judy, Judy" thing. He said, "I've never worked on a movie where the girl's name was Judy, and I've never said that line. Who is this Judy, Judy, Judy?" I told him it was Larry Storch who started it. Larry was one of the stars of the television show *F Troop,* and he was a pretty good impersonator too. In fact, he was one of the first to impersonate Cary Grant. He came up with the line, because he just liked the sound of the name. "Judy, Judy. Judy." It sounded more like something Cary Grant would say rather than "Mary, Mary, Mary" or "Cynthia, Cynthia, Cynthia." It was that simple. Larry Storch made it up. Cary said, "Well, I'll keep looking for this Judy, Judy, Judy. Who knows? Maybe someday I'll find her."

I'd see Cary from time to time at charity events. We'd often go up to Denver, Colorado, where Marvin Davis held a big annual fundraiser for diabetes research. Cary would always be there. We'd gravitate to a corner and just talk and talk about anything — except of course, his movies — at least for a few minutes. One time at a benefit we both attended, we discussed the pros and cons of celebrity. "You can never escape from it, can you?" I asked. "Never," he said. "Do you like it?" I inquired. "I like the perks. It's nice to get in the front of the line, or get a good table," he responded. And yet, a lot of the time he avoided being in the public eye. He said that celebrities who complained about it just shouldn't go out in public. But of course, you have to — occasionally. He could never understand why people get so excited when they meet a movie star, why they put movie stars on a pedestal, why they treated them like gods. "We're really not that important," he said. "It's not as if we achieved something really earth-shattering. I can understand someone wanting to meet a scientist, a composer, a writer, or an artist, to get their autograph. That makes sense to me. But all we actors do is memorize lines, say those lines to someone else, and try to make it look natural. Doesn't take any great ability." "Well," I said, "Actually it does, Cary. It takes someone with your skill to make it *look* like an art." That got a little chuckle out of him. When I think of Cary Grant, I think of a tall, well-built man, with very bright, gray hair and a perpetual tan. I think of him laughing, shoulders shaking up and down. He did love to laugh. He enjoyed life to the fullest, and that's what I remember most about Cary Grant. I was proud to know him.

Oh, and remember those polls I mentioned? In 2005, *Premiere Magazine* compiled its own list of the 100 greatest movie stars. *Premiere's* number one movie star? Cary Grant.

Burt Lancaster

One of the Best

I only met Burt Lancaster a few times, and he was always extremely nice to me. I met him once backstage at *The Dick Cavett Show*, and another time on an airplane. We were both sitting in first class, and we talked for about an hour. He was a great storyteller, and a charming man.

The third time I met Burt was on an American Airlines flight to New York. This time I was in economy, and he was in first class. I was surprised when the stewardess came up to me and said, "Mr. Little, I think your 'act' is in first class." "Which part of my act?" I asked. "Mr. Burt Lancaster." She agreed to allow me into the first-class section, and there he was, larger than life. I asked him if he remembered me, and he said, "Oh, sure. You're the guy who does me. Sit down. Am I still in your act?" "Of course," I said, "Always." "You know, I should charge you every time you do my voice," he said. "But Mr. Lancaster, think of all the publicity I give you. I keep your name out there," I exclaimed. "That's right," he said. "Then it's I who owe you. Let me upgrade you to first class." And he did! We talked movies for the rest of the flight. He asked if I did Gary Cooper. "Yup," I said as Gary Cooper. "Say something else as Gary Cooper," Burt said. "Nope," I said, again as Gary Cooper. Cooper's an easy one to do because he doesn't say anything!

Burt told me about *Vera Cruz*, a picture he'd made with Cooper. "When I read the script, I thought the role was perfect for John Wayne. He and I would be a good contrast. But he wasn't available, so I suggested Gary Cooper. I sent Coop the script, and he said, 'Yup, I'll do it.' I had pages of dialogue to deliver, and all he had to say was, 'I guess so,' and 'Really?' and 'See you later.' I thought I was acting him off the screen, because he didn't seem to be doing anything. But when I saw the rushes, I realized how wrong I was. He was born to be a movie actor. You couldn't take your eyes off him. Did you see the movie, Rich?" As Gary Cooper, I said, "Yup. It wasn't bad." Burt said, "I know it wasn't a classic, but it was a good action picture." I paused for a second, and then as John Wayne, I said, "It could have been better, pilgrim!"

The last time I saw Burt was in Atlantic City, New Jersey, while he was making a picture called, oddly enough, *Atlantic City*. It was probably his last great film, and he received an Academy Award nomination for it. I happened to be performing there at the time, and I heard they were shooting out on the Boardwalk at the crack of dawn, so I got up early and went to the set. Burt was standing around waiting for the crew to set up the scene, and it was *cold*. Boy, was it cold! We warmed our hands on our coffee cups, while he said to me, "You know, I've won an Oscar and I've made a lot of money making some pretty great movies. Why am I standing around here freezing to death?" I said, "You're acting, which is what you love to do." He looked at me and said, "You're absoutely right. Once an actor, always an actor." We stood around for another half hour or so, and he finally said, "I'm going inside. I'm tired. Rich, if they need me, you can imitate me. You finish the scene." And he walked away. That was the last time I saw him.

Burt built an incredible body of work. He was another actor who stretched himself, who didn't play the same role all the time. Although he was at his best when he was playing the macho, know-it-all man of steel, he could also play more subtle roles like that of Robert Stroud, in *Birdman of Alcatraz,* or columnist J.J. Hunsecker in *Sweet Smell of Success*. He had a tremendous range.

Bing Crosby

The Caring Crooner

*W*ho was the greatest entertainer of all time? Bing Crosby. Not because I knew him, not because I liked him, not because I thought he was a great actor or a great singer, but because the facts say so. He had 41 number one hits – The Beatles had 27, Elvis Presley had 18. He sold more than 500 million records. He made more records than any other singer, ever – four hundred more than Sinatra. He had the most popular single record ever, "White Christmas," which hit the charts 20 times. He was number one at the box office for five years, surpassed only by Tom Cruise at seven (but Bing is still the only star to hold the number one spot for five consecutive years). He was nominated for an Academy Award three times. He won once for *Going My Way*. He was a major radio star longer than any performer – 31 years. And he excelled in radio, television, movies, recordings and live performances. I can't think of any other entertainer who was as consistently popular in all five types of media.

Bing Crosby was a very special person in my life, and not at all the kind of person you'd imagine. He was very laid-back, nowhere near as exciting as, say, Frank Sinatra, but a real pro and a very bright man. From a very young age, he knew exactly where he was going and that nothing could stop him. He was one of the very few entertainers I've met in my life who was more concerned about how *you* would come off rather than how *he* would come off.

Bing was a very shy, humble man – at least that's what he wanted you to think. But he tended to exaggerate his humility. He couldn't handle compliments too well. All his life, he heard people say how great he was, so I guess after a while he started to downplay his importance, because it threw people off. Of course, he knew he was the best. All he had to do was take a look at his trophy room!

Bing also came across as not being very affectionate – no touching, kissing, or hugging. I once hugged him on *The Merv Griffin Show* and he

Merv, Bing Crosby & me on
"The Merv Griffin Show": 1965

seemed very uncomfortable. (Actually, I was just trying to find his wallet!) Because of his lack of outward affection, people thought he was cold and aloof. Not true! He had a very kind heart. But if you were a phony, or if you gushed all over him, he'd turn you off in a hurry. He loved his family, but he also loved to take off with Phil Harris for long fishing and hunting trips, leaving Kathryn to deal with the house and the kids.

Phillip Crosby, one of his sons from his first marriage, said, "He was a very caring father. I have nothing but the fondest memories of my dad. Going to the studio with him, our family vacations at our cabin in Idaho, going boating and fishing. That's what I like to remember." This is quite a different story from that told by Gary, Bing's oldest son, who published a book in 1983. He claimed Bing beat him and his brothers (twins Phillip and Dennis and Lindsay, the youngest,) and laid down strict rules with an iron fist. Phillip says this is not true. "Bing was strict, but he never beat us black and blue, and Gary was a vicious no-good liar for saying so. He wrote that book out of greed. He just wanted to make money. His career was going nowhere, he was an alcoholic, and he knew that humiliating our father and blackening his name was the only way he could sell books."

It's unfortunate that this image of Bing has stayed with many people who don't remember the sweet, gentle side of him as I do, but instead, choose to believe that he was a child abuser. No one ever paid attention to Phillip's denials after Gary's book came out. Phillip said, "My dad was a hero. I loved him very much, and he loved all of us, including, I'm sorry to say, Gary. He was a great father." He was, moreover, a truly great father to his second family.

I first met Bing in the late '60s. Georgie Jessel, who had been a big vaudeville star and was an actor and a singer, was doing a number of roasts on television. By this time, he was primarily known as "Mr. Toastmaster General" for his endless appearances at roasts and benefits. I don't imagine that too many people today remember him. Anyway, he was doing celebrity roasts on television long before Dean

Me with Bing Crosby on George Jessel's "Here Come the Stars" show: 1966

Martin. They were syndicated, one-hour, black-and-white shows. The show was called George Jessel's *Here Come the Stars.* I don't know how many he did, but I appeared on three of them: Jimmy Stewart's, Bing Crosby's, and Glenn Ford's. They weren't exactly roasts as we know them today. They were more like tributes to the stars. There was a dais, but there were also many things that weren't part of the usual roast – like singers performing, and comedy routines done away from the panel. Bing was the roastee, and I was very privileged to be on the dais. Phil Harris was there. So was Dorothy Lamour, and several other celebrities associated with Bing. I did a silly routine about Bing going to a haunted house and drinking a potion which turned him into a monster: Ed Sullivan. It was a pretty lame excuse for doing voices, but it went over quite well. If you look at the still photo taken at the time, however, you can see that no one else was too interested in what I was saying. This always happens at these roasts. While others are speaking, you're going over your own lines in your head, or reading your notes, so you're only half listening. I noticed this every time I did a roast – from Georgie Jessel right through to Dean Martin. However, I do remember Bing being very gracious, very charming, and very complimentary at that first meeting.

Ken Barnes, Bing Crosby, Gord Atkinson & me at one of Bing's recording sessions: 1976

The next time I met Bing was in January, 1976. Bing was recording four songs with a live, 40-piece orchestra at the United Western Studios on Sunset Boulevard in Hollywood, California. My Canadian friend, Gord Atkinson, and I were invited to watch Bing record, and stay for lunch. This was the first time I met Ken Barnes, who was producing the album, and who became a life-long friend. There are several things I remember about that session. After Bing sang a song called "Children," he came back into the control room to listen to the playback, but he kept his back to us. I noticed that he took out his handkerchief and started to dab his eyes, pretending to blow his nose. Everyone was happy with the playback except Ken Barnes. He asked Bing if he would do another take, but Bing said, "No, that one was fine." He was stubborn like that. It was, indeed, technically fine. The orchestra was perfect, and Bing sang the song beautifully. But Ken felt that he should have held the last note a fraction longer. So Ken suggested they redo just the last four bars, which they could then edit into the end of the song. Bing shook his head. "No, let's get on with the next number." He turned and headed back to the studio, and we saw tears in his eyes. It was then that it dawned on me that perhaps the lyrics reminded him of the trouble he'd had with his four sons from his first marriage.

I also remember the lunch we had at the studio. Bing was at one end of a long table, and I was down at the other end. I said to Bill Putnam, the studio director, "I wonder what it would take to get Bing to do my TV show?" Bing overheard me and said, "Pick up the phone and call." I pretended he wasn't listening and said, "Okay, do you happen to have his telephone number?" Bing said, "His telephone number?" Bing quickly shouted out the number. I called his office the next day, and he agreed to do my television show. It was quite a feather in my cap. When I told my producers, Al Rogers and Rich Eustis, that Bing Crosby had agreed to do my show, they got quite excited and went to tell NBC. The NBC guy said, "Well, we've got *Starsky and Hutch* that week. We'll have to bump them." And Rich Eustis said, "So?" The NBC guy replied, "Well, I don't know." He thought for a minute, "Bing Crosby. What's he done?" Rich Eustis was stupefied. "Would you like me to back up a truck with his credits?" In spite of that ignorant NBC executive, Bing did the show, and it was one of the best of the season.

What I remember most about Bing is how easygoing he was. Nothing seemed to faze him. During the show, we did a 10-minute medley in which I did Carol Channing, Louis Armstrong, Gene Kelly, Dean Martin, and Frank Sinatra. Bing sang in his own voice. I was scared to death; not only because it was Bing, but because at that time I wasn't very musical, and I kept making mistakes. We'd do two or three singers, and then I'd

Me & Bing Crosby on my TV variety show "The Rich Little Show": 1976

make a mistake. I'd come in wrong, or fluff a word, and then we'd have to do it over. This didn't seem to faze Bing. But after the first time, I really started to get concerned. On the next take, Bing fluffed. He did it deliberately. I thought, "Oh, he's made a mistake, just like me. So he's human, just like me." That put me at ease, and we finally got through the medley. Every time I made a mistake, Bing made a mistake. Later, I mentioned this to other performers who had worked with him, and they said, "Yeah, Bing would do that."

We did one really hilarious sketch on the show. It was a takeoff of Bing Crosby. We wanted to make fun of Bing's speaking pattern, particularly the 'B's' that he was known for. Charlotte Rae, a very talented actress who was a regular on my show, played Bing's mother. I played Bing and Bing played Bing's father. Joe Baker, a wonderful, little, chubby, British comedian, played Bing's son.

Charlotte Rae opened it with, "Well, Bing, breakfast is before you." I said, as Bing, "I think I'll have some brown bread and butter, or a baked bagel and a bowl of bouillabaisse before departing." Then Bing came in as Bing's father, "Ho, ho, ho, what a beautiful, blissful, balmy day. I'm bent on batting the ball around." Then in walked Joe Baker who, in a very English voice said, "Morning chaps, what's up?" We all looked at him and said, "B-b-b-boo, b-b-b-boo, b-b-b-boo." Joe Baker looked at the camera, started to cry, and said, "I wish I were Bob Hope's son!" It was a very cute little sketch, and the rehearsal seemed to go well. But half an hour before shooting it with a live audience, Bing walked into my dressing room and said, "I don't think we're going to be able to do that b-b-b sketch." "Why not?" I asked. "I can't get the hang of it." "Bing, you're great in it." "No, no. I'm not doing it as well as you guys. You guys are marvelous. I just can't do that b-b-b thing." "But Bing, we're doing you!" I explained. "Well, can you go over it again with me and show me how to do it?" he asked. "You want me to teach you how to do yourself?" I inquired. "Now don't get smart with me," Bing said. "Just tell me what you think." And we stood there in my dressing room and he did it perfectly. "Not very good, huh?" he asked. I replied, "Bing, you do yourself perfectly!" But he was still concerned about it. Of course, it was one of the highlights of the show, but I felt he was never really comfortable with it.

I've already mentioned what kind of man Bing was, and this was certainly verified when my brother Chris and his wife came in from Canada the same night Bing was taping my show. Neither of them had ever been to Los Angeles, so they were looking forward to seeing as much as possible. Bing was in the corner of the dressing room, writing something at a little table when Chris and his wife came in. I introduced them, then Bing went back to his table as Chris and I started chatting.

Chris told me they planned to go to Knott's Berry Farm the following day, about thirty miles outside of Hollywood. He asked if I could give him directions, which freeway to take, which exit ramp to take, where to park, how much it was going to cost to get in, what gate he should go to. I'd only been there once, years before, so I didn't have answers for him right away. We decided we'd have to call Knott's Berry Farm for directions. (Remember: this was before MapQuest or GPS.)

While we were in the middle of this discussion, none of us had noticed that Bing had left the room. About 10 minutes later, he walked back in with a piece of paper on which was written the entire itinerary. He had called Knott's Berry Farm and had the exact route from Hollywood, the correct exit ramp, the correct entrance gate, the entrance cost, and the parking details. He had even drawn a map. Not only that, he'd written down the names of a couple of people Chris and his wife should see when they got there. He'd overheard our conversation, and he just went ahead and took matters into his own hands. It indicated what a thoughtful man he was, and I was very moved that a man of his stature could be bothered with such trifling things.

Ken Barnes told me a story very similar to the Knott's Berry Farm one. The mother of one of Bing's musicians had travelled a great distance to London simply to watch Bing record, but she missed her connecting train and was held up at the station. She phoned the studio, but the session was over. Bing overheard her son on the phone telling her how well things had gone, and how sorry he was that she couldn't make it. Bing picked up the phone, told Ken to play the music back in the studio, and sang the song live for the woman over the telephone. Ken said he wished he could have taped it the second time, because Bing sang it with more feeling than when he'd recorded it the first time.

In 1981, four years after Bing passed away, I traveled to his Alma Mater, Gonzaga University in Spokane, Washington, for the unveiling of a bronze statue of him on the campus. Gord Atkinson was the emcee for the ceremony, which took place outside the Crosby Library, and he did a magnificent job. Kathryn Crosby, Bing's wife and a dear friend of mine, was there, as were other family members, political figures, and other friends of Bing, including Phil Harris, and songwriter Jimmy Van

Heusen. We all said a few words about Bing. It was a wonderful afternoon. I recall literally thousands of fans, not only in front of the stage, but hanging out of the dorm windows all around us.

I returned to Gonzaga one more time in 2003 to celebrate Bing's centennial, at which time they rededicated the statue by adding a plaque. Gord Atkinson was once again the master of ceremonies, and Kathryn Crosby was there, as was Frank Sinatra, Jr. The weekend consisted of seminars and lectures and several other very appropriate events. We all had a great time.

I consider myself privileged to have known Bing Crosby. He was not only a peerless entertainer, but also a fine and caring man.

Ed Sullivan

A Star with No Talent!

"Ed Sullivan will be a star, as long as other people have talent."
− Fred Allen

Ed Sullivan was a man who would try counting up to three, and get two of the numbers wrong. As an entertainer, he was a bit of a joke. Whenever young people ask me if Ed Sullivan was a big star, I'd reply, "Yes, he was a huge star on television. But he couldn't sing, he couldn't dance, he couldn't tell jokes − he could hardly talk! But he couldn't quit, because he was a star." Ed did have a couple of things going for him, however. First, he didn't have to do much. He simply had to introduce the acts, and then read a few questions to them after they had performed. Second, he had the best possible time-slot − eight o'clock on Sunday night. For most of his run, he had no real competition. His was a tightly-paced variety show, which were very popular at that time. If you didn't like what you were seeing one moment, chances are there'd be something you liked better five minutes later. The pace was fast, and there was something for everyone. Watching *The Ed Sullivan Show* on a Sunday night was a family ritual − everyone with a television set watched Ed. He mixed his show lineup pretty well too − singers, dancers, actors, comedians, ventriloquists, impersonators, jugglers − you name it. Any act worth its salt − and some that weren't! − appeared on his stage. Perhaps the most crucial factor of his success was that people could identify with him. They could picture themselves in his place. When he screwed up, mispronounced a name, or fumbled an introduction, he was funny. It was like your old Uncle Charlie trying to host a TV show.

If I had to name the three shows that made my career, I'd say *The Tonight Show, The Dean Martin Celebrity Roasts,* and *The Ed Sullivan Show.* Basically, three good appearances on Ed Sullivan made you a household name in America. That could never happen today. Even the most popular shows, like *American Idol*, attract far fewer viewers each week than Ed did.

Here's a confession: I didn't particularly like Ed. To be honest, I was afraid of him. He wasn't a very warm individual, he wasn't a kind person, and he had very little sense of humor. The only time he ever smiled or laughed was when everyone else was smiling or laughing and he didn't want to seem uninformed or square. To be fair, I did hear he was a much nicer person in his private life, and if you went to dinner with him – which I never did – he could be quite pleasant. One of the biggest problems on his show was that he was uptight all the time. The show was live, and he was under great pressure. Like any live show, things were always going wrong: artists didn't show up on time, microphones didn't work, sets became stuck, artists were in the wrong spot, or cue cards were wrong – things like that. Ed wasn't an ad-libber, like a Milton Berle or a Jackie Gleason; so most of the time, he just looked confused or disoriented. He used a lot of profanity, and boy, did he have a temper!

I always felt he didn't like it when impersonators did him. He pretended to, though, because the cameras were on him. But how could he really enjoy it when he saw an impersonator make him look like a buffoon – always screwing up words and phrases, hunkering over like a turtle, and saying stupid things? Ed had a lot of pride, and this must have affected him. But to his credit, he never let the viewers see his hurt. Most impersonators mimicked him – Will Jordon, who was the best, John Byner, and Jackie Mason – but my impersonation of Ed was probably the tamest of all. I tried to do him very precisely, with very little exaggeration. Ed went ballistic when he thought Jackie Mason had given him the finger on television. Jackie's take-off on Ed was hilarious. He would spin around like a top and exaggerate everything. I know Ed hated it, so I think he used the finger episode to ban Jackie from the show for several years. And just so you know how out to lunch Ed was, I can tell you that Jackie didn't even use his middle finger!

The first time I met Ed Sullivan, I was 18 years old and with my partner Geoff Scott. We'd been doing a lot of television in Canada, and thought we were pretty hot stuff. So, we went down to the Canadian

Me & my partner Geoff Scott meeting Ed Sullivan – Toronto: 1956

National Exhibition in Toronto determined to meet Ed Sullivan, who was doing a variety show there. We somehow managed to bluff our way into his dressing room. When we got there, we went right into our act.

Ed was on the phone at the time and didn't pay any attention to us. We were standing there doing our routine like we were on his show, but, unfortunately, we were imitating Canadians that he didn't know. He talked on the phone throughout our entire routine. He was just about to have us evicted from the room – these two annoying teens – when he suddenly noticed a reporter from the Globe & Mail newspaper. The reporter happened to know who Geoff & I were and what we were doing, so he said, "Can I get a picture?" Ed put his arm around us and said we were terrific and would like to book us on his show in ten years! This was really a brush-off, though we didn't realize it at the time. The headline in the paper read, "Sullivan tells Ottawa boys to come back and see him in a decade." This got him off the hook and made us happy, even though he had no intention of booking us on his show. But I fooled him. I did his show eight years later, even though it was without Geoff. He had no clue that I had already auditioned for him years ago in Toronto.

I'd made many appearances on *The Ed Sullivan Show*, the first of which was in the mid-'60s. I'd just come off *The Judy Garland Show*, and I was feeling pretty cocky and full of myself. Next up: *The Ed Sullivan Show*, which could make or break an entertainer's career. Even though I'd chosen a routine I'd done before, and knew where the laughs were, I worked on it over and over for days. I was determined to be absolutely perfect for my appearance. The night of the show finally arrived. I stood backstage watching the other acts, and I didn't feel particularly nervous. Then came my big moment. Ed announced, "Ladies and gentlemen, I'd like to bring out a young imper… impro … pro … per … comic, who comes to us from beautiful downtown Canader, making his very first appearance here on our show. Let's have a big U.S. welcome for *Little Richard*!"

Me with Ed on "The Ed Sullivan Show"

Well. I just stood there in disbelief! I guess that's me: *Little Richard*??? I didn't know what to do. The audience applauded as I stumbled out on the stage, looking for all the world like a deer caught in headlights. I lost all my confidence. I started into my routine, as if by rote, but all I could think was, "He introduced me as Little Richard!!!" My timing was way off. I just couldn't concentrate. I thought, "This is it. Back to Canader for me!" Suddenly, I realized that if I didn't do well, they wouldn't blame me. They'd blame Little Richard! I got a new burst of enthusiasm and finished the routine as best as I could. I got a pretty good reaction, but not what I'd hoped for, and left the stage. Ed usually stood on the side of the stage and watched the performers as they did their acts. He hardly ever went off stage. I was hoping he would go off during my routine, so someone could tell him my name was Rich Little. But he just stood there. To make things worse, as soon as I finished my routine, he strode back on stage, and said, "Now there's a fellow who's going places…Little Richard!" I went back to my dressing room feeling confused and angry. I didn't want visitors, but when I heard a knock on my door, and I opened it, Ed was standing there – very embarrassed. "I'm so sorry I screwed up your name. I didn't mean to. It was printed wrong on the card." I knew this wasn't true, but what are you going to say to Ed Sullivan? "Oh, that's all right Mr. Sullivan. We all make mistakes." He continued, "Tell you what, youngster. I want to make it up to you, so come back in two weeks, and do the show for us again. I'll get it right next time." I promptly said, "Of course, Mr. Sullivan." "Well, I'm very, very sorry this happened, Tiny, but we'll correct it in a couple of weeks." (That's not true, he didn't call me Tiny…but he could have.) Anyway, I went back in two weeks, and this time he did get my name right. I had a much better show. Although, I must tell you, standing in the wings for the second time, I had flashes of him calling me "Buddy Rich" or "Chicken Little."

Ed started out as a columnist for the *New York Daily News* and was very widely read. He usually wrote about show business, and that's why he was considered a natural to move into television. Everyone forgot, however, that the man had no sense of humor, could not ad-lib, couldn't talk without stumbling, and couldn't read. Either he had poor eyesight, or he was just not a good reader. I don't know which it was or if it was a combination of the two. Ed had cue cards for everything. Even his "ad-libs" were written down. Before the show on Sunday night, it took three boys to haul the cue cards on stage and pile them in the corner. For an average show, there must have been about 600 bits of cardboard piled up. The letters were printed about a foot high, so only a handful of words fit on each card. But even that didn't seem to help – he still screwed up. He didn't know about periods or commas, and he just stumbled through certain words and certain names, hoping they'd come out right. But usually they didn't. I'm sure he never rehearsed with those cue cards. I guess he felt he didn't need to.

The first great *faux pas* I heard about Ed was the night he came out on stage, strained at the cue card to decipher the words, and announced, "Tonight we have on our show an old-time singer who was popular in World War Eye." This was so typical of Ed. It became a kind of joke in the industry. There were so many great stories about Ed Sullivan, some of which I can even verify, because I was there. Others have been recounted by people like Jack Jones, Steve Rossi, Marty Allen and others. Everyone had a Sullivan story. One night at the home of singer Jerry Vale, Ed, Jerry, and I were standing on the back porch overlooking the yard. It was all dug up because Jerry was putting in a swimming pool, so there was this big hole in the ground. No one said anything for a moment or two, and then Ed came out with, "You know, Jerry, I like it. I really do. But I think it would look a lot better if you just put some water in it." Jerry and I both laughed – we just thought he was being funny. But Ed just stood there looking down at the huge empty hole.

Ed Sullivan & me doing a skit on "The Kopykats": 1972

Another time I was backstage at Caesars Palace in Las Vegas. Ed had just finished his show, which consisted of him pointing at his acts for two hours. Steve Lawrence and Eydie Gorme were there, and Ed asked us if we'd like to get a little late supper. Steve replied that we'd love to, but we were all invited to a party over at the McDonald's, and we felt we had to go. Obviously, Ed had nowhere to go, and he looked a little hurt. "Who are the McDonalds?" Ed asked. Steve said, "Oh, Bob and Patricia. They live in Spanish Trails." Ed said, "Not Robert and Pat McDonald?" "Yes," said Steve, "Do you know them?" "Do I know them? They're dear friends of mine!" Ed exclaimed. "Well, then," said Steve, "why don't you come along with us? I'm sure they'd love to see you." So we all piled into Steve's car and headed out to the McDonald home. We walked into the foyer and took our coats off. Ed walked over to a man standing nearby and hugged him, saying, "Bob, how nice to see you again. You look wonderful, just wonderful. Where's Pat?" Steve looked stricken, and said, "No, no Ed. Bob is over there. That's the butler you're hugging." Ed looked surprised, then said, "Well, I know that! I just haven't seen this butler in years."

One time Ed had a group of paraplegic veterans in his audience, and decided to introduce them. On live television, Ed's introduction went like this: "Ladies and gentlemen, in our audience tonight is a group of paraplegic veterans from St. Joseph's Hospital here in New York City. We're delighted to have them here. Guys, would you stand up there and take a bow?" Of course, these poor unfortunate men couldn't stand. A couple of them tried to get up, but fell into the aisles. Then Ed made things worse by continuing, "Where are they? On your feet youngsters!" The audience didn't know whether to laugh or cry. I know…it's a very sick story, but it actually did happen.

Another time Ed had Jose Feliciano on the show. Feliciano was blind, and Ed, going off the cue cards for a few seconds, announced, "We're going to bring out Jose Feliciano. He's an incredible, incredible talent. And the amazing thing about him, not only is he blind, he's Puerto Rican!" Classic Ed. Not only that, but Ed was standing backstage with Jose during the commercial just before he went on. He said to Jose, "Does…does the guide dog do any tricks?" Jose said, "Not that I know of, Mr. Sullivan." "Well, too bad. We could…We could have him do a spot."

On another show in the early '60s, Ed's major guest of the night was Sister Luc-Gabrielle, better known as the Singing Nun. She came on *The Ed Sullivan Show* to sing her huge number one hit song, "Dominique." She sat on a stool in her habit, strumming her guitar, and sang the song. She got a huge round of applause, because it was a very popular song. Ed came out and had his usual struggle with his cue cards. Why anyone thought he would be able to pronounce her name is a mystery for the ages. "Sister Lu…Luck…Lug…The Singing Nun, ladies and gentlemen! Isn't she wonderful? Wasn't she great? You know, for her performance tonight, we're going to give her a Jew!" Then there was a *long* pause. Ed looked bewildered, squinted at the cue cards, and said, "I'm sorry. A Jeep." Classic Sullivan.

When I first started doing Sullivan's show, I was still living in Ottawa. The show was on a Sunday, so I'd fly from Ottawa to Montreal, (a 20-minute flight), then I'd transfer to another airline in Montreal, fly into JFK Airport (another hour and a half), then take a cab to the Ed Sullivan Theater on Broadway before checking into the hotel.

Why I didn't do this all on a Saturday instead of the day of the show, I just don't know. I'm sure the show would have paid for two nights at a hotel. (I don't know…maybe not.) Anyway, if they wouldn't, I should have paid for the extra night myself. It would have been worth it, because the consequences of not making the show were unthinkable. You had to be there for a four o'clock rehearsal; if you missed that, you could still do the show by giving a verbal rundown of your act. However, this was only acceptable under "uncontrollable circumstances." I remember many Sunday mornings starting out from Ottawa in a blinding snowstorm. Both the Ottawa and Montreal flights would always be delayed, and when I'd finally arrive in New York, it was always a nightmare getting a cab. Still, I never missed a show, although I came close. I was a nervous wreck. Twice I arrived at the theater at 7:40 p.m. Ed was annoyed, as well he should have been. My agent was frantic, and the booking agent had no sympathy at all, even though two feet of snow had fallen on New York. I had to run through my act verbally with the stage manager. The cue card boys frantically scribbled down my monologue, while the makeup people threw powder on me, and I looked around for a steam iron for my clothes. While all this was going on, I'd go through my routine for the censors, who kept telling me over and over, "You can't say that! Find another word." Then I'd stand around waiting for Ed to okay my routine. All this would happen in about 20 minutes. How I ever gathered my composure, I'll never know.

One time, Ed booked too many acts for 60 minutes, but he was trying to fit them all in. After rehearsal, he said to me, "Ricardo, speed it up, will you? You have to knock three minutes off your routine." I said, "Ed, the whole bit is only five minutes. I was promised eight minutes, and now it's down to five. I don't mind that, but there's no way I can get it down to two minutes! You tell me what I can cut out."

He couldn't. He thought about it for a few minutes, then in desperation, he said, "I don't know…take out the impressions?" He was serious, but everyone standing around thought he was joking. It got such a big laugh that his mood changed, and he said, "Oh, all right. Keep it like it is. We'll cut down the roller skaters." He was referring to a comedy team from Canada called Wayne & Shuster. This one time they appeared to be doing a take-off on an ice hockey show, but because they were on a stage and not a hockey rink, they had to wear roller skates instead of ice skates. So, Ed only ever thought of them as roller skaters. (By the way, for all of you trivia freaks, Wayne & Shuster made more appearances on *The Ed Sullivan Show* than anyone except Ed himself. They were on a total of 58 times.) A couple of months later when I was making another appearance on the show, Wayne & Shuster were also coming back for another sketch. Ed was sitting next to me in makeup, and he turned to his director and said, "When do the roller skaters arrive?"

The worst time I ever had with Ed was when I tried to do a routine called "the bottle bit." I'd done this routine in my nightclub act and on *The Jackie Gleason Show*, and it had always been well received. I thought it would be perfect for Ed's show. I had about 12 small bottles filled with colored water: blues, greens, yellows, reds, browns. On each bottle, I had the name of a Hollywood star or a politician. The idea was that I would mix certain colors together in a glass, then drink it. As I mixed and drank, I would change from voice to voice. So, I started by imitating, say Jack Lemmon, and then added a little Gary Cooper. I would slowly turn into Jimmy Stewart, and then I'd add a little Humphrey Bogart, and a dash of Boris Karloff – to become Ed Sullivan. I thought it was a pretty clever routine. But Ed did not. "That's awful," he said when I did it for him for the first time. "It looks like you're drinking urine! And why would Boris Karloff turn into me? I don't even know Boris Karloff. He was a Democrat. I won't have you doing that piece of crap on my show. Find something else." Now this was at seven o'clock on Sunday night, and I had one hour to come up with a whole new routine. I was crushed, because I knew this routine would work. But for a moment I thought, maybe he had a point? Maybe it did look like piss. I was finally convinced a few weeks later when I was at Chicago's O'Hare Airport at carousel # 6 waiting for my luggage. Suddenly, one of my bags started down the moving carousel, and to my horror, the bag was half open. Little colored water bottles started sliding all over the place. People began to pick them up. "I got a John Wayne over here!" "I got a George Burns!" It was embarrassing beyond belief. They thought I was a doctor to the stars, and these were specimens! By the way, Truman Capote was pink.

Back in the '60s and '70s, Ed Sullivan was a gold mine for me. He was one of my most requested impressions of all time, right up to the time he passed away. Even today, he still gets a big reaction. He was on TV every week, and just about everyone watched him. He was larger than life, with a lot of idiosyncrasies. Hunched shoulders, always a scowl on his face, always tugging at his tie, always pointing to the act he was introducing. And, he used the same phrases over and over: "A really big shew!" "Let's hear it for them!" "Did you enjoy that?" People always tried to make Ed laugh, always tried to please him, because he had a lot of power. He could make or break a star. He liked to make you believe he was an authority on show business, especially since he inherited the nickname "Mr. Show Business." And yet, he seemed to be one sandwich short of a picnic, a little out of focus, and vague a lot of the time. I'm not saying he was stupid. On the contrary, he was extremely bright, but only about certain things. Ed just didn't think things through, and the mouth often started before the brain kicked in.

The last time I saw Ed Sullivan was not long before his death in 1974. I hadn't seen him in years – his show had gone off the air in 1971. I was walking across Fifth Avenue in New York City. I looked ahead of me, and there was Ed Sullivan walking toward me, very slowly. He was getting on in years, and as he approached, I thought, "He probably won't remember me." I recalled all those times I did his show, all the *faux pas* he'd made, and how he struggled with the cue cards. Even though I was pretty convinced he wouldn't know who I was, I said, "Hello, Mr. Sullivan." He looked very confused, and as he turned around, I thought, "Is he looking for cue cards?" He looked me up and down and then he said, "Fine. Fine." And then continued walking on. For a brief moment, I thought he was going to look at the flashing sign behind me and say: "Don't walk." Then I would have had yet another typical Ed Sullivan story.

All in all, Ed had a fantastic career. There was hardly a person in America who didn't know who he was, yet he was totally unknown to the rest of the world. He was a glorified emcee. He was a pointer who pointed at acts and struggled with cue cards. But he brought some of the greatest performers who ever lived onto his television show every Sunday night, and he will always remain one of the most interesting (if not talented) people I've ever met.

Dean Martin

Mr. Happy-Go-Lucky

"What kind of man was he?" "Did he drink as much as we think he did?" These are the two things most people want to know when I talk about Dean Martin.

Well, he was difficult to figure out. Off stage, he wasn't terribly outgoing. He wasn't a great conversationalist, but he was very pleasant, and he loved to laugh. He got a kick out of me, because I wasn't the usual stand-up comedian. I didn't tell jokes and I didn't do one-liners, but there was a lot of humor in what I did. Dean appreciated that. He loved it when I imitated people he knew, like Jimmy Stewart, John Wayne, and, of course, Frank Sinatra. I think Frank was fascinated by Dean because of his great humor and his terrific ability to come up with something funny at the drop of a hat. He was never stuck for an answer.

I never really got to know Dean on a personal level – we never had dinner together or anything like that. But I did appear on 24 of *The Dean Martin Celebrity Roasts* back in the '70s, and that's when we'd get to talk. We had several brief conversations, but he wasn't a sociable guy. He was a man of mystery. No one knew too much about him, and he kept his personal life very private. He did what he wanted to do, and he didn't care if people liked him or not. He was a bit like Robert Mitchum in that way. They both sailed through life doing pretty much what they pleased – no bullshit, no entourage. I never saw Dean upset. If he was mad about something, or if he didn't like the way things were going, he'd just walk away. That's what he ended up doing with Jerry Lewis.

As to the second question: Did he drink a lot? I'd say he was a pretty good drinker, although I never saw him tipsy. Well, to be honest, I did see him inebriated once, at the first Reagan Inauguration where Frank Sinatra took him off the show. Other than that, he just exaggerated his drinking image. He certainly didn't drink as much as Frank or Sammy Davis.

Having worked with both Dean Martin and Jerry Lewis, I can understand why they broke up. In fact, I'm surprised they stayed together as long as they did. It was probably the money, because they were very successful as a team, but their personalities were totally different. Jerry had a huge ego and was a workaholic and a perfectionist. Dean just wanted to get the job done as quickly as he could. He didn't like to rehearse. "When do you want me, what do I have to do, and when can I go home?" That was Dean. His main interests were golf, drinking (although, as I've said, he never drank as much as people thought he did), and watching old movies on television, particularly Westerns. He just loved Westerns and made a few of them himself.

I'm told he was very professional on the set – knew his lines, was liked by his co-stars, took direction, and didn't complain. But everything with Dean was speed. He was pretty lazy, actually. He didn't do well with actors or directors who wanted to do take after take. I think that's why he got along with Frank so well. They both had the same attitude – get the shot and move on. One can only shudder at the thought of a director like William Wyler working with both Dean and Frank. That movie would never have been finished. Wyler was famous for doing a lot of takes.

Working on Dean's variety show, which I did back in the seventies, was a very interesting experience. You rehearsed all week, but you never saw him. You did your entire act with a Dean Martin stand-in. The first time I did the show, I kept asking myself, "When is Dean going to do this?" Well, it turned out you'd be lucky if he did it when you taped it! You'd only get one take, so you'd better know what you were doing. My recollection is that we rehearsed for four days with the cast and the stand-in, then on the day of shooting, we'd run through everything again. Dean would arrive at NBC, go up to his dressing room, pour himself a drink, sit down on the sofa, and watch his stand-in do this last rehearsal. He'd get a feel of what was supposed to be happening, and then he'd go and do the show. The second he got the okay from the producer, he was out of there. So, he was probably not in the studio more than five or six hours, tops. Performers who were invited back for multiple appearances were those who could adjust to Dean's way of working, because it was obvious that he wasn't going to adjust to anyone else's.

Dean was also very lucky as a performer, because he could get away with what, frankly, could only be called sloppy work. Because he hadn't rehearsed all week and had only seen his double run through it, he'd sometimes get the moves wrong or say the wrong lines. Instead of doing it over, he'd just make a joke out of it, and the audience just loved that. He needed to make mistakes come off as funny, because he had an incredible way of recovering from them. He knew how to poke fun at himself, and sometimes it would end up funnier than if we'd done it correctly.

Dean, Kermit & me on "The Dean Martin Celebrity Roast": 1984

For the celebrity roasts, mostly at the old MGM Grand in Las Vegas (now Bally's), all Dean had to do was show up, get dressed, and walk onto the dais. An hour and a half or two hours later, he was finished. It was probably the easiest job any entertainer ever had. I remember one time we met in the green room. All the performers were milling about, chatting, drinking coffee, and getting ready for the taping. Dean walked in, and we chatted for a while. Then the producer, Greg Garrison, said, "All right everybody, take your places." We all walked backstage to our designated spots, so that we'd be in the correct seats on the dais. Dean turned to me and asked, "Who are we roasting tonight?" I said, "Excuse me?" "Who's the honoree?" He had no idea who we were roasting *two minutes before the taping started*! I said, "Michael Landon." Dean replied, "That's a good choice. This should be fun. I like him."

The "roastee" was of no importance to him; he just read the cue cards. And, because he hadn't read them beforehand, he made a lot of mistakes. Sometimes he could correct himself and make it funny, whereas other times, we knew it would have to be done over later. When the taping was done and everyone had left, Greg Garrison would stand beside the cue cards, and Dean would do all his introductions over again until the pronunciations and the inflections were perfect. That took a while, because by the time the show was over, Dean was pretty tired. But Greg also knew that if Dean totally ruined an introduction, and there was no way to recover, they could take something from what he did later. Before the taping, we were told not to read the cue cards while Dean was talking, because it looked bad. The cards were huge, and we were always tempted to look at them to see how he was butchering his words. Generally speaking, we tried not to look in that direction. If you think about it, he could have saved himself a lot of work by spending half an hour or so running over the cue cards before we started taping. But he just didn't care.

Dean Martin, Frank Sinatra, Milton Berle & me – Wonder what I was saying that kept them so interested?

As Dean got older, his energy level decreased, and he didn't want to work as much. I think he would have retired much sooner, but the people around him knew that if he kept performing, it would give him something to do and prolong his life. This was especially important after he lost one of his sons in a plane crash. The truth is, though, by that time, he'd become even lazier. I'm told that one time when he was doing his act at the MGM Grand, about three or four years before he died, the program manager said, "Dean, your shows are too short. People have paid a lot of money to see you, and you're only doing thirty-five minutes. You've got to do at least forty-five. There've been several complaints that the show is way too short." So, instead of adding a couple of extra songs, he took the fast-tempo song "Bad, Bad, Leroy Brown," which was a long number anyway, and slowed it down to a ballad! The original was probably about three minutes. By the time Dean finished with it, it was about eight minutes. That was his only concession. And, if you do the math, you'll see that it still didn't bring him up to the 45 minutes the management wanted!

Dean always came across as the happy-go-lucky, fun-loving guy, just sailing through life without a care. But that wasn't really the case. There was a lot of sadness in Dean Martin, particularly near the end of his life when he was slowing down. When Frank Sinatra took him on that last tour with Sammy Davis, Jr., Frank wanted to rekindle the old Rat Pack days; the days when they'd do the shows, have fun, and stay up all night drinking and carousing. Sammy went along with it, but not Dean. By this time, Dean just wanted to get through the show, watch television, and play golf. He didn't want to socialize; in fact, he really didn't want to do that tour at all. He mentioned this to Frank several times, but he let Frank talk him into it. It was too bad, because things were pretty much over for Dean by that time. It wasn't a fun tour, and one night Dean just got on a plane and went home. Liza Minnelli finished the tour for him. Frank was quite upset, and they didn't talk for a while. But Frank should have understood that Dean didn't really care and hadn't wanted to go in the first place. Sometimes, it's better to take "no" for an answer. Although Frank was a superstar, Dean, in many ways, was really more successful than Frank. He had more hit records and was a success in television, which Frank wasn't. Admittedly, Frank's music is more popular today, however, than is Dean's.

Toward the end of his life, Dean just became a shell. He ate dinner alone every night at his favorite restaurant, La Famiglia. Occasionally, one or two of his friends would stop to say "hello" or come up to speak with him. He would say, "How are you, pallie?" He was always very polite, but he'd never carry on a real conversation. His spirit had just kind of drifted away. That boisterous, enthusiastic, happy-go-lucky guy was kind of a lost soul at the end.

Carol Channing

Hello, Dolly!

arol Channing is an absolute delight. She's a perfect subject for an impersonator: larger than life, very identifiable, with a very distinct, high-pitched, raspy, little voice. I've met her many, many times over the years and we've always had a very good rapport. She absolutely loved my impression of her, and I did it at every opportunity. She opened for me in the '80s at the Sands Hotel in Las Vegas, and then I came out and we both sang "Hello, Dolly!" together. She started it, then I did her, and then I ended as Louis Armstrong. The audience loved it.

Me & Carol Channing

Carol is one of those show biz people who makes you smile at the very mention of her name. I'd put her in the same category as Jimmy Durante or Louis Armstrong or Maurice Chevalier. People just love her. Although she's primarily known for her stage work, her face and voice are instantly recognizable, and whenever I imitate her on stage, I get a tremendous reaction.

She was married to Charles Lowe. He died when they were in the middle of a divorce, but he was always with her in the days when I was friendly with her. He'd sit out in the audience for every performance – when I was on, *not* when she was on! His favorite impression of mine was Jimmy Carter. He'd just stamp his feet and scream every time I did it. Once, I asked him, "What's with Jimmy Carter? Is he a friend of yours?" And he said, "I just love the way you do him. He reminds me of Howdy Doody."

One evening, after attending the theater in New York, my date and I ran into Charles and Carol in a restaurant. They invited us to join them. Now in those days, Carol was not eating regular food. She had with her jars and bags of organic food – things like seaweed and other strange-looking stuff in bottles. She'd proceed to take out her food and put it on her plate. We all looked on and thought, "Yuck! How awful looking!" Well, apparently, she thought so too, but this was all she was allowed to eat – or so she believed. Four or five bottles of this stuff were on the table when our food arrived. She looked over and said, "Oh, what did you order?" My date said, "Pork chops." "Oh, they smell so good! What are you having, Rich?" "Chicken pot pie," I answered. "May I smell it?" I let her smell it. Eventually, the waiter came over to take our dessert orders. Carol asked, "Can I order for you?" I wondered why, and she added, "I just like to say the sounds of the food." As I recall, she finally kicked that phase and started to eat regular food again. Thank heaven. All she'd do was spend the whole time asking people at various tables what they were having. "I can't eat it," she'd say, "but I like to talk about it."

Charles, Carol, and I were quite social back in the late '70s and early '80s. One night, we were working together at the Sands Hotel, and we were invited to go to the late show at Caesars Palace. Carol said, "I'll wait for you, and we'll go together." So I finished my show, and we dashed over to Caesars. Now, Carol was always a little overdone – you know, huge eyelashes, a lot of makeup, flashy clothes. She really stood out. We got out of the limo and headed toward the main showroom. As we walked through the lobby, people recognized us and called out, "Hi, Carol!" Well, she was recognized – no one paid much attention to me!

One guy just stood there with his mouth open. "Oh, my God!" he said, "This is terrific! Oh, Carol Channing, right?" She just looked at him, trying to move on. "Oh, my God, I've seen people do Carol Channing before, but I've never seen anybody do her this good. Are you in *La Cage*? Are you in the Frank Marino show? This is the best female impersonation I've ever seen! Who are you fella?"

Without batting an eye, Carol said, "I'm a truck driver from Toledo, and I just came in third in the Carol Channing look-alike contest." And then she swept on. As we departed, I heard the man mumbling, "Wow! That's the best Carol Channing look-alike I've ever seen."

Edward G. Robinson

Deaf as a Post

*B*efore I tell you about Edward G. Robinson, one of the giant tough guys of his era, let me take a short detour to let you know how I met him. Back in the '60s, Bob Barker hosted a very popular television program called *Truth or Consequences*. (That was a long time ago, when Bob had dark hair!) I was invited on the show to "do Mr. Magoo." The gag was that they would blindfold a woman in the audience and have her guess which of three voices was Mr. Magoo. Jack DeLeon, a well-known impersonator of the time, was the second voice. The third, of course, was Jim Backus. Ouch! I had to compete with the guy who was the voice of the real Mr. Magoo! I'd been doing Mr. Magoo in my nightclub act for years, and as a result, I had some really funny lines already prepared. But Jim Backus wasn't a stand-up comedian, so he just did the voice, saying something simple, like, "Oh, you're a beautiful woman. It's nice to be here …" or whatever. Jack DeLeon's Magoo was nothing to write home about. So, of course, the contestant picked me as the real Mr. Magoo, because I was funny. Everyone was stunned. The lady was embarrassed. I was embarrassed. I was a better Mr. Magoo than Mr. Magoo! Jim took it pretty well, and we stayed in touch. A couple of months later, he invited me to his birthday party. That's how I came to meet the great Edward G. Robinson.

Jim and his wife, Henny, had a beautiful home in Brentwood, California. There were hundreds of people at the party, including many very important people from the film industry. As I was mingling, someone came up to me and said, "You've got to meet Edward G. Robinson, because you do a great impression of him."

Well, this kind of thing has happened many times in my life. It can be amusing, but it can also be terrifying. I was dragged over to Edward G. Robinson, who was standing in the middle of the living room with a drink in his hand. We were surrounded by a huge crowd of people, all chattering away. There was plenty of liquor and a lot of laughter. Over the noise, someone said, "Mr. Robinson, I'd like you to meet Rich Little." He looked up and said, "Who?" "Rich Little, the impersonator." He looked at me for a moment, and then he beamed – what a relief that he recognized me! He must have seen me on television. "He does an impression of you. Would you like to hear it?" Edward's smile got wider, and I was really on the spot. There were three problems. One, the room was way too noisy for me to do an impression. He would never hear me. Two, he was hard of hearing – I could see he was wearing a hearing aid. And three – you guessed it – "What am I going to say? What am I going to do?" I had learned one of the famous speeches from *Double Indemnity*, one of the greatest roles he ever played, so I knew I could do that. The problem was I didn't think he'd be able to hear it. Edward G. Robinson's is not a very loud voice, particularly in that role. I could, of course, do *Little Caesar*, or I could just yell. I realized I was in a ridiculous position, but he kept looking up at me and saying, "Let's hear it, let's hear it." No one had stopped talking, but they all turned around to see what was going on. He motioned me to get on with it, and I realized I had no choice now. I had to do something. As I started to do the impression, I thought, "I really don't have to talk. I just have to move my lips and do the gestures, because no one can hear anything anyway." I began the speech, "Walter, the first thing that struck me in the Dietrichson case was the suicide angle, but I threw it in the wastepaper basket 10 seconds later." It was so noisy, I couldn't even hear what was coming out of my mouth, but I pressed on and did the whole speech. He never took his eyes off me. I did all the gestures, all the mannerisms, which certainly helped, but I knew that with the noise level, and him being hard of hearing, it was a futile gesture.

Finally, he must have noticed that my lips had stopped moving, and a couple of people trying to listen over the din applauded. He just beamed and applauded like you wouldn't believe. He kept giving me the okay sign, and he kept clapping. He was just thrilled. Obviously, he was being polite, or maybe he just liked the gestures, or he felt he had to react because people were looking at him. But for me, this was not one of my finer moments. I barely heard him say to the person next to him, "That was absolutely superb!" And then he walked away. Several people later told me that he was thrilled to meet me and said I'd done the best impression of him that anyone had ever done. So I guess I scored big with Edward G. Robinson by being a failure. Just think of how it would have gone over if he'd been able to hear me!

Glenn Ford

A Strange Star

I'd heard many things about Glenn Ford before I met him – mainly that he was a little strange. I don't say this as a put-down – we're all a little strange at times. But, I'd heard that his behavior could be slightly bizarre, and I certainly can bear witness to this. Let me say first, that he was always very, very nice to me; always very sweet and kind, and certainly one of our great movie actors. I watched him recently in an old Western, *3:10 to Yuma*, and he was absolutely brilliant. He could certainly underplay beautifully.

The first time I met Glenn was back in 1968 on George Jessel's *Here Come the Stars*. Glenn was the honoree. I can't tell you what I did at his roast, because, honestly, I can't remember. But I do recall that a comedian by the name of Joey Villa (a friend of mine who passed away in 2005 in Las Vegas) was one of the performers on the show. He was a pretty hot comic back in the '60s. Now, Joey didn't know Glenn Ford, so he wrote a routine about cowboys and Indians, which was a good way to go, because Glenn had done a few Westerns. For some strange reason, Glenn was at the rehearsal, perhaps checking up on what people were going to do on the show. He was always a bit insecure. Joey ran through his routine, which I thought was very funny, as did everyone else. But Glenn, seated in the front row, was outraged. He stormed up on the stage and went after the producer. Right in front of Joey and everyone else who was sitting around (including me), he started putting Joey down. He said, "That is the worst routine I have ever seen! It's degrading, it's disgusting, it's not funny, it's a put-down of Indians, and I will not have it on any show that I'm on!" The producer responded, "What are you talking about? It's very funny." "No, he's making fun of the Indians, and I know a lot of Indians. I have a lot of close friends who are Indians, and I will not have them put down in that way. I want him thrown off the show!" Joey just stood there, not saying a word. He was probably in shock. Everyone else was kind of stunned. Glenn went on to say how great the Indian people were, how we had taken their land away from them, and now we're making fun of them. The producer kept saying, "But it's a comedy routine. It's just jokes." To which Glenn said, "Well, I don't see it that way, and I want him off the show." We were only a few hours away from taping. Finally, the producer, in desperation, said, "Wait a minute Glenn. You should talk! How many Indians have you killed in all the movies you've made?" Well, that stunned him. I watched his face turn red. He paused and said, "Well, that's true. But I used blanks!" We all had to turn away because we were laughing hysterically, but Glenn didn't see the humor, and he just walked away. I never forgot that incident. And whenever I saw Joey Villa after that, I'd remind him of it. He'd always say, "That was the most bizarre thing I've ever seen." Incidentally, Joey did not do the show. Perhaps Glenn used that excuse because he couldn't think of another comeback.

Me & Glenn Ford on my variety show: 1976

Glenn was my guest star on *The Rich Little Show* back in the '70s. I was thrilled to have him on the show because I'd admired him as an actor for years, but I didn't really know him. We ran through some of the sketches we were going to do, and Glenn was excellent. The show was due to shoot at 7:30 p.m., so around six o'clock, we broke for dinner. Glenn came up to me and said, "Rich, the audience is pretty close to the stage." I said, "Yes, it's a very small studio. The stage is small, so we put the audience up really close so you can see them in almost every shot." He asked, "How close are they?" "Well, I don't know exactly. The front row is a few feet from the stage." "Do you know the exact distance?" "No. Is it that important?" "Well, I just want to know how close they are, 'cause, y'know, I'm a movie star and I never work in front of an audience." I said, "Glenn, you don't have to worry. They'll love you, and the material is pretty good." He repeated, "Yes, but I have to know how close they are." "Well, I would guess about three feet from the stage." "Oh, okay." Then, he disappeared. At about a quarter to seven, just before the audience was due to come in, I saw Glenn with a tape measure, carefully measuring the distance from the seat in the center of the front row to the stage – and he was writing it down. A couple of us backstage started to laugh, but I think he was afraid of the live audience. I don't know if he thought they were going to hit him or what, but he really needed to know how far away they were.

"To my good friend Rich with all my respect and admiration. Sincerely, Glenn 1980"

Although these are two slightly bizarre stories, I don't mean to say that Glenn was strange all the time. He wasn't. He obviously reacted to pressure differently than most of us. He took himself very seriously, and was always, as I said, very nice to me. After the show, he signed a picture for me, which I still have. He also wrote some very flattering things about me. And that's what I remember about Glenn Ford.

Jimmy Stewart
A Perfect American

I will always have a special place in my heart for Jimmy Stewart. He was the first movie star I ever impersonated, so I took quite a shine to him. I saw Jimmy Stewart not only as a great action hero, but as a very fine actor. I watched all of his Westerns: *Winchester 73, Bend in the River, The Naked Spur, The Man from Laramie*. I remember really liking *The Far Country* when I saw it at the Capitol Theater. I even went back and saw it a second time. Jimmy starred with Walter Brennan and Ruth Roman. It was a good cowboy movie, a little more advanced than the Allan "Rocky" Lane movies I'd left behind! After seeing the movie twice, I started to do my impression of Jimmy Stewart. I drove my folks crazy — I wouldn't talk in my own voice any more, only Jimmy Stewart's. I'd say to my mum at dinner, "Can I have a piece of apple…p-p-pie?" The word "pie" was perfect for Jimmy Stewart. It was so perfect, that in real life, he named his horse Pie. Then, I had an idea to tape *The Far Country*, so that I could study Jimmy's voice — audio only, of course, because this was before videotape. I had just acquired a reel-to-reel tape recorder, which I'd paid for with money saved from my paper route. I made good use of this machine. I would tape all of my favorite radio programs — *The Lux Theater, Suspense, The Fat Man, My Favorite Story with Ronald Colman, The Shadow* — I had quite a collection of radio shows. It was a very cheap machine and had to be plugged into the wall — there was no provision for battery power. When the reels wouldn't move, I would just bang on it. Obviously, the only way I was going to be able to record the dialogue of *The Far Country* was by going back to the theater with my tape recorder. I picked a Wednesday matinee after school, when hardly anyone was in the theater. I smuggled my little tape recorder into the Capitol Theater, found an outlet under the screen, plugged in the machine, and started taping the movie. This, of course, was highly illegal, but I did it anyway. I even changed reels, but no one seemed to notice. There was no one around at first, just a few people in the back, but then the theater started to fill up a bit. I began to watch the movie for a second time, and then around six o'clock or 6:30, I decided it was time to go home. So, I proceeded to rewind the tape back to the beginning. I'd left the volume up on the machine by mistake, so as I rewound, chipmunk sounds filled the theater. This created a huge stir, with people yelling and screaming, "What's going on? Are there mice in the theater?" The ushers came running down the aisle and saw what I was doing. I grabbed my tape recorder and my reels, and they yanked me out of the theater and threw me into the street!

In the late '60s when I performed on George Jessel's *Here Come the Stars* honoring Jimmy Stewart, I made up and performed a speech from one of his movies, *Anatomy of a Murder*. It was a kind of double-talk speech that told the whole plot of the film in about ten sentences. It made no sense at all, but Jimmy got a big kick out of it. Then, I did Jimmy singing "People," the famous Barbara Streisand song from *Funny Girl*. I'd started doing non-singers singing, and this seemed to get a big reaction. I did John Wayne singing, Ed Sullivan singing, Huntley and Brinkley singing, Claude Rains singing, Cary Grant singing – people who weren't known for their singing, trying to sing and doing it seriously. I picked "People" for Jimmy Stewart because it had a lot of high notes. I kind of talk-sang it, and then sang at the end, where it goes, "People, people who need people, are the luckiest people (long pause) …in the world." Jimmy loved it. After the show, he told me, "Rich, you do me pretty good singing." I said, "You've gotta be kidding me." He said, "No, no. If I did it, it would be worse. When I sing in the shower, the soap gets up and leaves the dish." He actually did sing in one picture, MGM's *Born to Dance* (1936), where he sang in a park to Eleanor Powell. He said, "I kinda talk-sang 'Easy to Love,' and I worried more about that than anything I'd ever done up to that point in my career. But I got through it, and Eleanor Powell didn't laugh once! I put so much work into it, and I thought it came out pretty well. But the higher-ups at MGM thought it was terrible, and they got a professional singer to dub it. That proved to be even more ridiculous, because at the premier, here I was talking in my high, stuttering voice, and all of a sudden I started to 'sing,' and out came this big baritone voice. The audience just broke up laughing. So they went back to the original version with me singing, and that's the way the picture was released." Occasionally, he'd sing "Ragtime Cowboy Joe" and play the accordion on television, and sang a couple of songs in *Night Passage*, but that was about it as far as the singing went!

Me with Jimmy & Gloria Stewart

Over the years, we became fairly friendly and somewhat social. I'd run into him from time to time, usually at awards dinners where he was being honored. I was often invited along to do my Jimmy Stewart in front of him, which he never failed to enjoy. I'd see him at the American Film Institute dinners and various charity events, and I found him to be an incredible story teller with a great sense of humor. It might take him a long time to get the story out, but he was a natural born wit. And, of course, he was The Great American. He had a tremendous war record as a bomber pilot in the Eighth Air Force during World War II and flew many missions. His son was killed in the Vietnam War. He had no scandal ever attached to him and he was happily married to his wife, Gloria, for more than 40 years. He was a lovely man, easy to talk to, no airs at all, and totally down to earth. We'd sit around many nights and just talk about his career and the impressions I did, which ones went over, what I was currently doing of him in the act, and what people liked. Invariably, he'd say to me, "Rich, I don't need to work anymore. You're doin' it all for me. You're keepin' me alive out there." That was a nice compliment.

One evening, we were leaving the Century Plaza Hotel in Los Angeles after an AFI dinner, and hundreds of people were waiting for the valet parkers to bring their cars around. Jimmy couldn't find his ticket, and Gloria was getting a little impatient. A long line had formed behind them. Jimmy was giving the guy a description of the car and the license number, "M…three…seven…" when Gloria came up to me and said, "Rich, you do Jimmy. Would you please tell the fellow what our license number is?" She whispered it in my ear. So I said, as Jim, speaking fast, "M37648J." The guy said, "Thank you. Both of you," and ran across the street to get the car. Everyone standing around us was laughing.

In the '70s, I used to host *The Tonight Show* when Johnny Carson was off. This was a big thrill for me, because I got a chance to invite several of the people I impersonated on the show. I really wanted to have Jimmy Stewart on, so I phoned him up, and he said fine, he'd love to do the show. This was around Christmas time. We locked him in as a guest, but about a week before he was supposed to appear, I got a call at home, "R…R…Rich, this is Jim," and I almost said, "That's fair, but who else do you do?" I thought it was someone doing a bad impression of Jimmy Stewart when it suddenly dawned on me, "Good heavens, this is Jimmy!" I said, "Yes, Jim." "R…R…Rich, I'm afraid that with regards to *The Tonight Show*, I'm not going to be able to…to…to…" He was having such a hard time getting the words out, that I finished the sentence for him, in his voice, "… not going to be able to make it." "That's right, that's right, that's exactly right." Now that I was into imitating him, I couldn't stop. I asked, still in his voice, "Well, why not, Jim?" And he replied, "Well, the family's coming down for Christmas, and we've got too much going on and…and…it's just a bad time." Still imitating Jimmy, I said, "Well, don't you worry about it, Jim. I understand perfectly. Let's do it another time. I'll be hosting the show again in two or three weeks." "Well, great! I'm glad you understand, and I'm sorry I have to bug out on you." "No problem at all. We'll set it up for another time." I still hadn't stopped using his voice. He said, "F…f…fine." I replied, "Thank you, Jim," and hung up the phone. I found out later from Gloria that when he hung up, she asked him, "Who was that, dear?" and Jimmy's answer was, "That was Jimmy Stewart telling me he couldn't do *The Tonight Show*." What a sense of humor!

Another time, Jimmy and I were invited to do a radio show that was being recorded somewhere in Beverly Hills, California. I picked up

Jimmy at his home, and we drove down and parked about a block away from the building in which the interview was being held. As we walked toward the studio, every few feet someone stopped us and asked Jimmy for his autograph, made some comment, talked about one of his movies they'd seen, or just said how much they loved him. This was wonderful, of course, but it was taking us a heck of a long time to walk this one block. When we finally arrived at the studio and were going up in the elevator, I asked him, "Jim, boy, it must be impossible for you to go anywhere in public. You're so recognizable." "Yes, it can be a problem sometimes, especially if you're in a hurry, and you don't want to be rude to anybody. I developed a little gimmick that usually works." I asked what it was, and he replied, "Well, if I'm walking down the street, and I see someone walking toward me, and I get the feeling that they're going to recognize me, I just make a face when I get closer to them. I puff out my cheeks, squint my eye, and make a distortion with my mouth so that I look like Quasimodo. Then, they look close, and they think I'm some kind of disfigured person, and they just walk by." Once, however, this backfired on him. He saw a family walking toward him, so he did his Quasimodo face. When they got closer to him, the man looked up and said, "Jimmy, what happened to your face?" As it turned out, these people were friends of his, and the wife said, "Jimmy, were you in an accident?" Of course, Jimmy stopped when he recognized them and became his natural self. They looked at him in disbelief. Then, very slowly, very quietly, they moved away. Jim said, "I felt like a complete idiot. I wrote them a letter not long after that apologizing. I said I was working on a character for a movie, and I was just going through some of the facial expressions." I wondered what the movie would have been – *The Quasimodo Story?*

One day, I took Gord Atkinson, my closest friend from Canada, over to see Jimmy. Gord had a radio program in Canada on which he interviewed various celebrities. Over the years, I introduced him to a number of people for his show. On this particular afternoon, he was going to meet and interview Jimmy. We arrived at his house, Gloria invited us in, Gord did the interview in the backyard, we had tea, and just talked for a while. It was a lovely afternoon. As we were leaving, Jimmy walked us to

Jimmy Stewart & me at a charity event

our car, which was parked at the curb. All of a sudden, a bus came around the corner, packed with tourists. The driver was on a loudspeaker system, and he was saying, "Ladies and gentlemen, over to my right, we have the home of Jim … good heavens! There's Mr. Stewart himself, right there, coming down the path! And there's Rich Little with him too! My goodness, two celebrities at the same time!" Of course, everyone on the bus was very excited. The driver asked, "Mr. Little, what are you doing at Jimmy Stewart's house?" Jimmy, without missing a beat, said, "Rich comes by here twice a month just to get his batteries charged." I thought it was one of the funniest lines I'd ever heard, and I almost fell into the flower bed. Everyone on the bus flew into gales of laughter.

Another time I picked Jimmy up at his house for a charity event in Beverly Hills. He wasn't too thrilled to have to attend, but he'd committed himself, and Gloria didn't want to go. We drove over to the Beverly Hills Hotel, not too far from his home. We each gave a speech, and I did my impression of Jimmy. By then it was about eleven o'clock, and I was driving him home. He was either very tired or a little out of it, because he couldn't remember the street or where we were. He'd say, "Turn right here." So I turned right. "No, this isn't right. Go back the other way." So we went back the other way. "Make a left here." So I made a left. "This doesn't look right either." Finally, I said, "Jim, don't you know where you live?" "Wait a minute till I get my bearings here." I couldn't help thinking Jimmy was reliving *No Highway in the Sky*, in which he played an absent-minded scientist who was very vague and couldn't remember where he lived. I said, "Jim, are you reliving that movie?" He laughed and said, "I guess I'm becoming Mr. Honey-cutt again." Finally, he said, "This is it. Turn right here." And we pulled into the driveway. "Are you sure this is your house, Jim?" I asked. And he said, "Well, if it isn't, I'm gonna give them a helluva shock." As he approached the house, I yelled out, "If it's the wrong house, just make that face."

Jimmy Stewart & me at his home
on Roxbury Drive in Beverly Hills

Jimmy agreed to present me with a humanitarian award at an event at which I was being honored. He got up to the podium and said, "Y'know, Rich has been imitating me for years and years, and it's a perfect imitation. In fact, he does me better than I do, so I've been considering adopting him. But Gloria won't have anything to do with it. She said, 'One Jimmy Stewart going 'Waaal…waaal…waaal.' around the house is really all I can handle!' So we just forgot about it."

Jimmy loved practical jokes. If you were putting someone on, he'd pick up on it immediately and go right along with the gag. One time, we were waiting for an elevator with a whole bunch of people, and I decided to have some fun. When the elevator arrived, I walked on first, then Jimmy. But before anyone else could enter, I put my hand out and said, "Please wait a second until Harvey (the imaginary rabbit from the play and movie of the same title) gets on." Jimmy picked that right up and said, "Oh, Harvey! I didn't see you behind us. Would you just hold for second?" He motioned people back, and said, "Harvey, come get on the elevator." I moved back to give Harvey some room, and Jimmy sort of led Harvey onto the elevator, and said, "Are you okay, Harve? Well good. All right, now all the rest of you can get on." They did, but Jimmy kept a space open for Harvey. "You alright, Harve? Is anyone stepping on your foot? No? Okay, you can close the elevator now." The elevator door closed, and Jimmy talked to Harvey all the way up to the 20th floor. It was hilarious, because he did it entirely serious. Everyone in the elevator got a tremendous kick out of it, because most of them knew Jimmy and were familiar with the movie. But those who didn't know about it, probably thought Jimmy should be committed.

Me & Jimmy Stewart at a formal event

At one of *The Dean Martin Celebrity Roasts*, I told the audience that Jimmy Stewart was losing it. He just didn't sound the way he used to. I asked him to stand up. I said, "Jim, you just don't sound like yourself anymore, so maybe I should give you a few pointers." I told him, "Now the first thing you've got to do Jimmy, is you've got to bend over." So he bent over. "You've got to squint your eyes the way you do in your Westerns, and then you've got to put your hand out in that way that you do and kind of move it around." Jim was doing all this, but doing it very badly. He looked ridiculous. He was all hunched over, his eyes were half shut, he was waving his arm, and he said, "I feel terrible." I said, "How do you think *we* feel? We've been watching you for forty years!" Finally, he said, "Waaal…" And I said, "There's no hope for you at all!" "Pretty bad, huh?" "Awful!" I replied. "That's the worst Jimmy Stewart I've ever heard!" Then I got the entire audience to stand up, put their hands out, squint, and say, "Waaal…" I said, "See, Jim? Everybody in the room can do you better than you!" This got a tremendous reaction from the audience – and none of it was scripted! He just went along with the gag. Even though in those days, everyone stuck pretty close to the script. I'll bet that if any actor went off script, Jimmy would've kept right up with them, because he was a good listener and very much in tune with everything that was going on. As I've said before, the best actors are good listeners.

Gloria, Jimmy's wife, was perfect for him, because she was totally down to earth and could tell a phony person from a mile away. She always said exactly what was on her mind, and she had a great sense of humor. She always watched out for Jimmy and tried to protect him. When Jimmy stopped making movies, people wanted him to attend every major event in Hollywood, but she became very selective and turned many of them down. She once told me, "All Jim does now is accept awards. You do him so well, I wish you'd attend some of these events for him." She was great fun to be with. They both were. I knew that after Gloria died, it wouldn't be long before Jimmy would be joining her, because his whole life, really, was wrapped up in Gloria.

I once asked him if he had ever taken acting lessons. He said, "No. I just looked the other actor in the face and told him the truth. I always acted for fun. I got paid to wait."

Jimmy was a great man and a great actor. The American Film Institute voted him the third greatest actor of all time.

Stewart Granger

Take Him or Leave Him

O f all the performers I've known in my lifetime, none was more fascinating to me than the British actor, Stewart Granger: the great
swashbuckler of the '50s. This was a man Howard Keel described as "The
Slasher." The Slasher he was, in more ways than one. He was an angry, bitter, critical, belligerent, sometimes cruel, conceited, argumentative person;
but he never ceased to intrigue me. There was something about him that
drew you (or at least drew me) to him. He had presence; he had intelligence.
He could also be charming, kind and considerate – it just depended on his
mood. To be a friend of Stewart Granger's, you had to be a very tolerant
person. You couldn't let him get under your skin. If he said something very
hurtful, you just had to let it go. You could never remain his friend if you
were a sensitive person. Many, many people just couldn't tolerate him – they
didn't have the patience. I tolerated him for a couple of reasons. First, I was
a tremendous fan of his talent. As a kid, I idolized Stewart Granger. I became
an instant fan when I saw *Scaramouche*. I thought films like *The Prisoner of
Zenda, Young Bess, Harry Black and the Tiger*, and *Saraband for Dead Lovers* were
just tremendous. I had a *Life* magazine cover photo of Granger in *Scaramouche* tacked up on my bedroom wall, and I read everything about him in
magazines like *Photoplay*. I loved the stories about him telling off some co-
star or getting into an argument with a director. He was larger than life,
brash, and full of energy. That anger that he had inside of him really made
him what he was.

He was born in London as James Lablanche Stewart, but changed his
name so as not to be confused with the American actor, Jimmy Stewart.
Granger was his grandmother's maiden name. The public knew him as Stewart Granger, but all his friends called him Jimmy. He became a star in England in the '40s with such films as *The Man in Grey, Waterloo Road,* and *Blanche
Fury,* but many of these films didn't get universal distribution. The only one
of his English films that was a success in America was *Caesar and Cleopatra,*
but that was probably due to the drawing power of its stars: Vivien Leigh and

Stewart Granger & me

Claude Rains. Stewart Granger came to America in 1950 to make *King Solomon's Mines,* and that's when his entire life changed course. Even though he was a huge star in England, American audiences looked on him as an overnight sensation, and he rapidly became one of the hottest stars in the MGM (Metro-Goldwyn-Mayer) stable. No one had ever seen anyone quite like him, and certainly not from England! Britain turned out very few macho film stars. Richard Harris was one, Anthony Steele another, and of course, Sean Connery; but they all came after Granger had made his mark. *King Solomon's Mines* was the turning point. Even though he went on to make 30 or 40 more pictures after that, *King Solomon's Mines* remained his finest performance.

Unfortunately for Granger, he was one of the last of MGM's contract players, and he had to do pretty much whatever the studio dictated. Otherwise, he could be put on suspension without salary. For quite a while, he refused to sign a long-term contract, because he wanted to remain freelance. But he finally had to give in, and he never ceased to regret it. Though he got a plum role every once in a while, he also got a lot of pits as well. Even though he was tied to MGM, he sometimes made his own bad choices. He followed up *King Solomon's Mines* with *Soldiers Three,* which was a disaster. He went on to make *All the Brothers Were Valiant, The Last Hunt,* and *Green Fire,* all entertaining movies but not classics by any means. This bothered him greatly, and he often talked to me about what might have been. It was sad to see a man who was at the height of his career in 1951, realize, that by 1965, it was pretty well over. He became very bitter as the years went by, very disillusioned about growing older and about missing out on roles he could have done so well. He regretted turning down some of the roles that did very well for other actors. When he told Laurence Olivier how much he envied him for having played such roles as *The Entertainer* or

Richard III, Olivier replied, "Maybe so, old boy, but I could never have played *Scaramouche!*"

Granger talked a lot about a movie called *Mogambo,* which Clark Gable made with Grace Kelly in 1953. It was a remake of *Red Dust,* a film Gable made with Jean Harlow in 1932. It was Granger who had the idea to update *Red Dust,* which appealed to him very much, because it was set in Africa. He took the idea to MGM, and, of course, he assumed he would play the lead. The producer, his friend Sam Zimbalist, led him to believe he would get the role. Eventually, though, the studio executives came to him and said, "This is going to be a terrific film. Your career is going great guns right now, and we need a picture for Gable. The king is growing older, and he hasn't had many hits lately. He needs something to give his career a boost, and this is the perfect vehicle." So Granger had no choice but to step aside, and Gable got the picture. I once told him, "I thought Gable was pretty good in *Mogambo.*" "No, he wasn't," Stewart growled. "He was bloody awful. He wore big, baggy shorts and had knobby knees, and it ruined the picture." I said, "You know, even if you'd done *Mogambo,* it wouldn't have changed anything. It's not a classic movie by any means. It's nowhere as good as *King Solomon's Mines,* and it was directed by John Ford. I can't imagine you and Ford working together – neither one of you would have survived!" Indeed, John Ford was a tough, crotchety old filmmaker who made some of the greatest pictures in Hollywood history, but he was not an easy man to get along with, and neither was Stewart. I said, "Forget about *Mogambo.*" He exclaimed, "But it was my idea!" "So what?" I said. "It was your idea and you didn't do it. It won't change anything."

Granger also felt he could have played Burt Lancaster's role in *From Here to Eternity,* but it wasn't offered to him. I said, "Well, Burt was very good in that film." "Yes, but I would have been better," he replied. "But you're English," I pointed out. But he had an answer for everything. "So was Deborah Kerr. I can play an American just as well as she did."

One of his biggest disappointments was not doing *Ben Hur.* Marlon Brando was set to play Ben Hur, and Stewart was offered the role of Messala, Ben Hur's closest friend who later becomes his sworn enemy. Brando as Ben Hur might sound like a ridiculous piece of casting, but he was a huge star and very much in demand no matter what the vehicle. Brando fell out, however, and the next choice was Kirk Douglas, who was also a big star and a very accomplished actor. Stewart thought they would make a very powerful pair of enemies. But then Douglas fell out. The next choice was Charlton Heston. "Charlton Heston? Charlton Heston as Ben Hur? No way! He's the most boring actor on the screen. He's a stiff. He has no humor. He's never made a single great picture. I'm a much bigger star than he is. There's no way I'm going to play second fiddle to Charlton Heston!" Stewart ranted. His agent argued, "There's no reason for you to turn it down, Stewart. William Wyler, who's directing, has more Academy Awards than any other director in Hollywood. It's going to be one of the biggest pictures of the year – even of the century! It's the best thing you could possibly be doing right now." But Stewart said, "No. I'm not taking second billing to Charlton Heston." All his friends told him that he was making a big mistake, so he finally and reluctantly agreed to do the film. When he called William Wyler and told him he'd take the role, however, Stephen Boyd had already been cast. Of course, this was a major mistake on Stewart's part, because even though he made many good films, he never made a classic. *Ben Hur* would have put him on the map forever. This was just like Alan Ladd turning down the movie, *Giant*. A lot of actors used bad judgement.

Marilyn Ball (mother of actress Lindsay Wagner), Stewart Granger & me at Stewart's 75th birthday

I first met Stewart Granger in the early '70s. Mel Tormé called me one evening to tell me that Stewart Granger was coming to his house in an hour, and I was so eager to meet him. I was there in 10 minutes. Stewart and I hit it off immediately. In fact, we had

almost met a few years previously, when my then-wife, Jeanne, knowing how much I admired him, had the idea of surprising me on my 45th birthday by having him appear at a restaurant to wait on our table. She almost pulled it off, too. As Stewart confided in me later, he was tempted to do it because he was a fan of my work, but he was not comfortable in crowds and didn't want to be in a restaurant with a bunch of strangers. A couple of weeks after we met, Stewart invited me to his apartment in Palos Verdes, overlooking the Pacific. He lived in an Aladdin's cave of memorabilia. Huge posters from all of his movies lined the hallways, and trophies of elephant tusks and boar's heads from his various hunting expeditions hung everywhere, although he assured me he was a conservationist. He explained that in the '50s, several animal species needed thinning out, so he would only kill the old ones – this was his justification for having all those dead animals in his apartment.

Milton Berle, Stewart Granger, me, Norm Crosby & Mel Tormé
at my Friar's Roast – California: 1987

Granger would have a gathering every couple of weeks, surrounding himself only with people who held him in great esteem; people who were willing to listen to him hold court. Although he claimed not to like "yes men," you had to be very careful not to contradict him. He needed to be the center of attention and was very well-versed on numerous topics. But he was very opinionated on them all. He also loved tennis, which made for another common bond between us, but he had a problem in later years because he only had one lung. Earlier in his life, doctors in England had diagnosed him with lung cancer and had removed one of his lungs; only to discover that, in fact, he had tuberculosis, which could have been cured with drugs. He was very bitter about this, because he was very macho and very athletic, and his diminished lung capacity hampered him greatly. When we played tennis together, we would play doubles. (Less tiring for a man with one lung.) I'd hit the ball in the corner to win the point. He would be at the net, and he'd say to me, "What are you doing?" "Trying to win the point," I'd reply. "But you hit it in the corner?" Then I'd repeat, "Yeah, to win the point." "But I'm standing here. You should hit to me. That's rude!" he'd yell. "But I'm trying to beat you. That's the object of the game!" I'd exclaim. "I don't care. Hit it to me! Don't hit it over there. Can't you see I'm standing here? That's not polite," he would say. So, I would hit it to him and we lost every game!

My former wife, Jeanne, who is also English, was always a great fan of Stewart's, but she eventually lost interest in spending time with him, because he was so opinionated and arrogant. I just figured you had to take him for what he was, or not at all. As a result, I put up with a lot of abuse from him, although not as much as other people. He would needle anyone who contradicted him, and if he felt they just didn't know what he was talking about, he wouldn't invite them back.

One afternoon I took my friend Ken Barnes over to meet Stewart. Ken was an English record producer whom I had met when he was producing for Bing Crosby in Hollywood in the early '70s. Ken was thrilled to meet Stewart, but it all turned very sour over an argument about *The Prisoner of Zenda*. In the '50s, Stewart was in a remake of this classic movie of the '30s, which had starred Ronald Colman, David Niven and Madeleine Carroll. As trivia buffs will attest to, the remake was shot frame-for-frame with the original. Richard Thorpe, the director, simply had a Moviola machine on the set, which followed each scene, shot-for-shot. There were only a very few minor differences, but basically it was the same film with different actors. Ken told Stewart that he had run both movies at the same time and had found some significant differences. Stewart erupted, "No, there are no differences! It's exactly the same movie! Only the actors are different! I should know — I was in it!" So Ken went on to describe a scene toward the end of the movie in which Granger had a gun on one of the guards, and the guard had his hands up. The shadow of the guard could be seen on the stone wall, and Prince Rupert, (James Mason) could see this shadow. This is how he knew a stranger was in the castle. In the original version, the guard did not have his hands up. Now this may seem really trivial, but not to Stewart. He insisted that the guard had his hands up in *both* versions. Then said, "Rich, I invited your friend over here, he drank my wine, he ate my food, and now he's telling me I'm a liar!" I tried to make light of it by saying, "Well, he had his hands up because he was stretching," or something stupid like that, but it didn't calm Stewart down one bit. Things got a bit uncomfortable, so Ken and I left, assuring Stewart that we'd had a wonderful evening. Ken had a wonderful sense of humor, so shortly after that evening, he arranged to have a huge proclamation printed on a scroll of old English parchment, signed by the Prime Minister, and finished off with an official seal confirming that one version of *The Prisoner of Zenda* showed the guard with his hands up, and one didn't. Stewart was reluctant to invite Ken back to his apartment, but I assured him Ken just wanted to make amends, so Stewart finally agreed. Ken presented him with the scroll at the end of the evening, and everyone howled with laughter – except Stewart. He just gave a little grin. But I could tell deep down he was still very angry. I don't think he ever really forgave Ken for contradicting him. Stewart Granger was a man who knew how to bear a grudge.

Toward the close of the last century, when history still wore a rose and politics had not yet outgrown Richard Nixon, a Great Royal Scandal was whispered in the Anterooms of Hollywood. However true it was, any resemblance to Heroes, Villains, Actors or Directors living or dead is a coincidence that exists only in the realms of filmdom's folklore.

Proclamation

To the good people of Strelsau in the province of Zenda. Be it known that, according to Hollywood folklore, Mr. Ronald Colman has always been regarded as " the finest Elphberg of them all." However, a recent investigation calls this opinion into question and suggests that Mr. Stewart Granger may be more deserving of the title.

In 1937 when Mr. Colman's "Rudolph Rassendyll" broke into the castle of Zenda to free the captive King, he made the foolish error of letting the guard stand with his hands in the air. Thus betraying his position and forcing him to fight his way to the dungeon of the King. But, in 1952, Mr. Granger - playing the same role - took the wise step of making the guard put his hands down. Thus, avoiding immediate discovery. From this simple act of intelligence, the case for Mr. Granger is made.

However, when confronted with this fact, Mr. Granger stubbornly denied that he had done anything different to Mr. Colman. It was only when the two versions were screened side by side that Mr. Granger's superior intellect became clear.

(2)

But still the supporters of Mr. Colman claim that he is by far the nobler of the two and a true gentleman in every sense of the word while Mr. Granger lacks the charm and the culture so necessary to the story. But that's their opinion.

To plead the case for Mr. Granger, the Royal Court of Ruritania has called a State Banquet inviting two of Mr. Granger's most revered associates - film director, Compton Bennett (who directed Mr. Granger in "King Solomom's Mines") and Sir John Mills (an old friend and actor equally dear to Mr. Granger's heart) to step forth and testify on his behalf.

Of course, no one speaks for Mr. Colman because he and his associates have long since passed away. But, in true keeping with tradition, Mr. Granger's supporters say "The King is Dead. Long Live the King."

----

(3)
The Banquet
This momentous event takes place in the huge assembly hall in the opulent Castle of Strelsau Seating two thousand guests.

The Assembly President rises and in his vibrant voice calls for order and speaks

"Call Mr. Compton Bennett."

The Toastmaster Royal rises and speaks>

"Word has just come from England that yesterday, Mr. Compton Bennett collapsed during a heated exchange in a toilet on London's Clapham Common railway station. He was rushed by ambulance to the nearest hospital where he was pronounced dead on arrival. His doctor described his condition as "Satisfactory." Mr. Granger happily concurs, since it was he who generously paid Mr. Bennett's medical bill. As a result, Mr. Compton Bennett will be absent from this assembly. Permanently"

The Assembly President again rises and in his vibrant voice calls for order and speaks.

"Call Sir John Mills."

(4)

The Toastmaster Royal again rises and speaks.

"Sir John Mills is absent from this assembly having been ordered by Her Majesty The Queen to officiate at the opening of a new space-age Toilet Factory in his home town of Felixstowe, Suffolk where he once distinguished himself as a toilet paper salesman. For his services to the industry, the Queen has awarded Sir John the Royal Order of the Rolls."

The Assembly President concludes

"There being no witnesses to speak on Mr. Granger's behalf, I suggest that everyone continue with this excellent dinner cooked and prepared by Mr. Granger himself and to avail yourselves of the complimentary Sangria"

Epilogue

So is Mr Stewart Granger the finest Elphberg of them all ? Or do we defer to the long-held Hollywood opinion that this distinction belongs - as it always has - to Mr. Ronald Colman ?

This leaves but **ONE BURNING QUESTION** in the hearts and minds of the loyal populace of Strelsau - from the richest and most high-born of citizens to the poorest and most down-trodden of peasants

" WHO GIVES A SHIT ? "

Signed and sealed

By **King Rudolf V11** of Ruritania

Stewart was also very specific about his likes and dislikes. He didn't like David Niven, even though they'd been very close at one time. "We had a falling out," he said. He also had a falling out with Cary Grant and was very critical of him. I think he admired Cary, so goodness knows what happened there. He liked James Mason, who remained one of his closest friends. They made several films together and were in touch right up until Mason's death in 1983. He also greatly admired Robert Donat, the wonderful English actor who played Mr. Chipping in the original *Goodbye, Mr. Chips* and won an Academy Award for his performance. Their friendship went way back to the time they were both theater actors, and I believe Donat helped Stewart quite a bit in the early days of his career. His two favorite contemporary movie stars were Gregory Peck and Burt Lancaster, two of my own personal favorites. He said, "They have the best body of work of any actors on the screen. They've made more great pictures than any other actors of their generation – well, with the exception of a few duds here and there." As much as he liked Jimmy Stewart, however, he didn't like him in Westerns. "He's not believable in Westerns," he would say. "Too scrawny. You could knock him down with a feather." In response, I'd say, "You don't have to be a huge guy to be macho on screen." "Hah! I could beat up Jimmy Stewart with one hand!" Typical Stewart Granger. He didn't particularly like Jack Lemmon, either. "He's too affected. All that stuttering and stammering. It's all developed, all created." Agree with him or not, Stewart always had an opinion, and that's why I found him so fascinating.

Stewart had all his English movies sent to him from England on tape, but they were in their format, so he couldn't play them on his VCR. I took them all to a man in London who converted them from the English format to the American one. I had them gift-wrapped, and when I gave them to him, he lit up like a Christmas tree. He was so grateful – though, of course, I'd had copies made for me too! Now, together with his American films, I think he had almost all the movies he'd ever made on tape. I found it very interesting that he would critique them when we watched them together. I wish he were alive today to give his commentary on the DVD versions of these films! He loved to be interviewed, because he loved to be in the limelight and was flattered that people remembered him. I became very good friends with Sid Craig, his agent at the time, who also became my agent. Sid knew how to handle him, and sometimes Sid and I would gang up on him to get him to do something he was reluctant to do. Sid got him to do episodes of *Murder, She Wrote* and *The Love Boat*, and other popular shows of the time, just to get his face on the screen. This created an entirely new audience for him. After one episode of *The Love Boat*, the whole cast and crew gathered around to present him with a birthday cake and applaud him for ten minutes. He was hesitant at first to do this kind of work: "I don't want to do that. I don't like the script. It's not a big enough role. I don't like the billing. I don't like the cast. I don't think so-and-so is a good actor." But he finally got into the groove, and these appearances did a great deal to improve his morale.

Dinner at Stewart's house was quite a ritual. Cooking was one of the great passions of his life, and he would literally spend days preparing his dinner parties. One of the problems about being his guest, however, was that if you asked for seconds because the food was so good, he'd call you a pig. But if you didn't eat enough (according to his standards of "enough"), then he'd get mad at you for not appreciating his food. It was a very thin line to tread! One evening, when there were only three of us for dinner, I noticed he was cooking enough food for a regiment. "I know," he admitted, "I take the rest of this stuff down to the nuns at the convent down the road, and they love it."

Granger got a lot of fan mail, particularly from fans that saw reruns of his films from his swashbuckling days. Sometimes they didn't realize that he was now in his seventies. One particularly enthusiastic fan, who had been bombarding him with fan mail, finally came to visit him. She was in her twenties, and announced that she was staying for a week. On Saturday night, he threw a big party. The moment I arrived, I knew there was trouble. "Rich, she's driving me nuts! She's here for another three days and I don't think I can take it." "What's wrong?" I asked. "Oh, she's fussing around, bringing me things, waiting on me, tidying up all over the place." "Then tell her to leave," I suggested. "She can't," he said. "She's got the airplane fare locked in. Tomorrow she wants to go to the zoo! Then Friday we're going to Knott's Berry Farm, and oh my God, I just don't know what to do." I said, "Help her with her homework!"

He was in a terrible mood that night, and I remember it in particular, because it was the night he and I had a falling out. Sometime that evening, I threw out what I thought was a harmless barb, and he turned on me. In front of a roomful of people, he said, "Rich, you're vicious. I don't like the way you pick at people." He kept nagging at me like this, embarrassing me in front of everyone. I later realized that he was doing this because he was so unhappy at having the girl there for the week, but at the same time, I was really upset. I said to myself, "That's it! I've had it! Jeanne is right. He's just too hard to take. I can bend, I can take some of his criticisms, but this time he's gone too far. I'll just cool it for a while, just fade away." But I'll be darned if he didn't call me up to apologize as soon as I got home. It was about 11:30 p.m., and he said, "I'm so sorry. I'm in a really bad mood. This girl is driving me crazy. I don't want to lose you as a friend. I went too far. Please, please accept my apology." Of course I did. Then he said, "You wouldn't want to go to Knott's Berry Farm, would you?"

It was hard to be his friend, but I wouldn't have given up that friendship for all the world.

Rich in his first movie, a documentary, "Map & Compass" at age 12

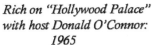

Rich on "Hollywood Palace" with host Donald O'Connor: 1965

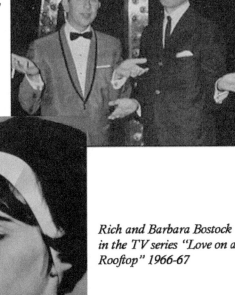

Rich and Barbara Bostock in the TV series "Love on a Rooftop" 1966-67

*Rich with Marlo Thomas
in "That Girl" 1967*

*(L-R):
Rich, Ruth Buzzi,
Barbara Feldon &
John on "The John
Davidson Show"
1970*

*Rich, Julie & Sammy Davis, Jr. on
"The Julie Andrews Hour" 1973*

"The Kopykats" cast: (L-R) Will Jordan, Frank Gorshin, George Kirby, special guest Ed Sullivan, Rich, Joe Baker & Marilyn Michaels

Phyllis Diller & Rich

Guest host Raymond Burr & Rich on "The Kopykats" 1972

*Rich with roastee
Kirk Douglas on
"The Dean
Martin Celebrity
Roast" 1973*

*Rich with Doris on the
"Doris Day Today"
show: 1975*

*(L-R): Fred
MacMurray, June
Haver, President
Gerald Ford, Rich
& Jeanne Little*

Ann Margaret, Perry & Rich on the "Perry Como in Las Vegas" special: 1976

Charlotte Rae, Dudley & Rich on "The Rich Little Show" 1976

(L-R): Rich, Julie Andrews, Bob Hope, Harry Belafonte & Alan King meeting Queen Elizabeth: 1977

Liberace,
Elizabeth Little
& Rich
(Liberace told
me, "Wipe that
mustache off!")

Jack Lord &
Rich on
"Hawaii Five-O"
1977

Rich receiving the AGVA "Georgie Award" from Ernest Borgnine: 1978

The cast of "The Dean Martin Celebrity Roast" for Frank Sinatra: 1978

Captains Rich, Marty Feldman & Gabe Kaplan in the NBC special "US Against the World" 1977

Loni Anderson & Rich
on an episode of
"The Love Boat"
1980

President Reagan's Inaugural Gala: (L-R) President & Nancy Reagan, Frank Sinatra,
Johnny Carson, Ben Vereen, Rich, Ethel Merman & President George H. W. Bush:
1981

Patricia Neal's
59th birthday
celebration:
(L-R)
Jillie Mack,
Tom Selleck,
Jeanne Little,
publicist Barry
Landau,
Patricia Neal &
Rich: 1985

First Lady Nancy Reagan with Santa (Rich) at the Reagan's Christmas event for children: 1988

Rich with Dolly Parton on her show "Dolly!" 1988

*To my terrific Rich —
who is anything but little —
love Claire —*

Rich with Claire Trevor

Rich receives star on the Canada Walk of Fame: 1998

Rich & Bob Hope

Jackie Gleason, Art Carney & Rich

Gregory Peck

The Dependable Stalwart

*M*y God, I've always been in awe of Gregory Peck. It was an absolute joy to meet him, and I wasn't disappointed. He was a very serious, deep-thinking kind of guy. He did have a sense of humor, but most of the time he took things very seriously. I met him a few times through Frank Sinatra – they were great friends – and he knew that I imitated him. Every time he'd see me, I'd have to do "him" for him, and he'd always say, "Ah, a little better than the last time." For some reason, Gregory Peck and I were selected to do some interviews for the 1984 Summer Olympic Games, which were held in Los Angeles. I have no idea why the two of us were chosen, but we went along to a press conference to talk about the Olympics. I think we both did a little fudging – I wasn't all that familiar with the Olympics, quite honestly, I love sports in general, but I'm not a particular fan of any specific Olympic sport. We both did our best, and told the press how great it was to have the Olympic Games in Los Angeles, how much revenue it would bring to the city, and how interesting it was to see the events live. After the interview, we sat down for a cup of coffee together, just the two of us. Peck didn't say much – he just kept staring straight ahead. I'd seen that look of his in many movies, so I kept silent. Finally, without looking up, he said, "I lied." "What?" "I lied." "You lied?" "I lied – not just once, but twice." I couldn't believe it. Gregory Peck a liar? Twice, yet! "What do you mean?" I asked. He explained, "I told them I was looking forward to the Olympic Games, that I was coming out to see all of the events, and that it was much better than watching it on television. I told them that the last time the games were held in Los Angeles, in 1932, I went to all the events with my father, that I was so thrilled back then, and I was looking forward to seeing the Olympics again – it would bring back so many memories." "Well that's great!" I said. "No," he continued, "it's a lie. I'm not coming at all. I find it a big bore. I may watch it on television, sitting by my pool, a drink at my side. As for the games I went to with my father,

I remember nothing, absolutely nothing. So I lied. Twice." I laughed, "Well, who cares? I kind of lied myself. I said I was coming, but I'm not." "Well, I guess we're both pretty good actors then, huh?"

Once I was playing tennis against Peck – I think it was a charity event – and he was pretty good. He hit the ball hard. I wasn't that great a tennis player, so I knew this was going to be rough. My solution? Every time I hit the ball over the net, and he went for it, I'd yell out the name of one of his bad movies. He'd get so distracted that he'd miss the shot. He was annoyed at this, but also kind of amused. Unfortunately, I didn't get many free shots from him doing this, because he didn't make that many bad movies. Once I'd gone through *Mackenna's Gold, Behold a Pale Horse,* and *Beloved Infidel,* I was stuck for another bad movie. If I'd yelled out *To Kill a Mockingbird, Twelve O'Clock High, Cape Fear* or *Big Country,* I would have been pounded into the dirt!

Near the end of his life, Gregory Peck did a one-man show in which he talked about his career, and showed some film clips. Many movie stars did this – I think Bette Davis was one of the first. Peck had been talked into it, and he told me he only wanted to play out-of-the-way places so he could talk to the people who would never have a chance to see him. He didn't want to play the big cities. Cary Grant did the same with his one-man show. On one occasion, Peck was in Rochester, New York, and I really wanted to see the show, so I flew up. I sent him a fax beforehand, telling him I was coming. I got a nice reply saying how thrilled he was that I'd come all that way just to see him and to be sure to say hello. My secretary and I flew up to Rochester, checked into the hotel, and that night we went to see his show. It was fabulous. His dialogue was superb. I don't know if he wrote it all himself, but there were some very funny and some very informative bits. He opened the show with a clip from *To Kill a Mockingbird,* the scene where a straggly looking dog is limping down the street, and Peck's character, Atticus Finch, grabs a gun. It's obvious the dog is sick, so he fires the gun, and his children recoil in horror. When the lights went up, Gregory walked out to thunderous applause, saying, "I did not kill that dog!" I enjoyed the whole thing immensely. After the show, he had a question and answer session. He had stock answers for most of the questions, since they're usu-

Gregory Peck, his wife
Veronique & me: 1997

ally pretty much the same: "Who's your favorite actor?" or "Who's your favorite leading lady?" or "What's your favorite movie?" Then I stood up, and he asked, "What's your question?" I replied, "Does anybody do a good impression of Gregory Peck?" Of course, the audience didn't know who the heck I was. He looked down at me and said, "Well, there's a fellow by the name of Rich Little. He does an impression of me, but I don't know how good it is." I said, "Rich Little? I can do it much better than him." "You can?" "Of course. His impression of you is terrible." "Well, let's hear it," he said. So, I did the "Duty, Honor, Country" speech, which I'd memorized from *MacArthur*. I did the whole speech very dramatically, just like he did it in the movies. When I finished, the audience broke into applause. He stared at me with that Gregory Peck look, and said, "I think you'd better come backstage after the show. We're going to have to work on that." "Oh, okay," I said, and we subsequently visited backstage for quite a while. It was a great thrill for me to do my impression in front of him and to get such a great reaction, because he really did like it.

That was the last time I saw Gregory Peck. He was the greatest listener I'd ever seen on the screen. In acting, it's often the reacting that's so important, listening to what the other person is saying. That's what acting is all about: looking someone in the face and telling them the truth. That voice of his, along with his incredible talent and his good looks, made him a superstar. Films such as: *To Kill a Mockingbird, Gentlemen's Agreement, The Stalking Moon* and *The Gunfighter* didn't hurt any either.

He was a remarkable man, and it was a privilege to have known him.

Howard Cosell

The Man We Loved to Hate

*H*oward Cosell was, to put it mildly, an interesting personality. He was almost a put–on, a man not to be taken seriously, although he desperately wanted people to do just that. He was a great impression for my act. Almost everyone back in the '70s could do impressions of Howard Cosell, even women!

Many people thought he was arrogant and pompous and didn't know what he was talking about. But I thought he was very knowledgeable, especially when it came to sports. He was very controversial and very full of himself. He entered a room voice first. When there was nothing more to be said, Howard was still saying it. It's true that at times he was a bit of a pain, and his ego certainly was out of control, but I found him quite interesting and very funny. I liked him, and I think he liked me.

Me & Howard Cosell

Howard was always full of enthusiasm, but you could never be sure just how he was going to react to anything. At the height of my career, back in the '70s, I was headlining at the MGM Grand in Las Vegas. One night, he burst into my dressing room, singing "New York, New York," the Frank Sinatra song. He didn't say hello or anything, he just kept singing. I stuck out my hand and said, "Hi, Howard." He just went right on singing. He did the whole song, getting most of the lyrics wrong, but bellowing, "Aaaaaand if I can make it here, I'll make it anywhere…" It was a really bad impression of Frank Sinatra, and totally off-key, but he went through all of Frank's moves, skipping around the room and snapping his fingers. As soon as he finished the song, he started it again. I realized he'd just returned from a concert of Frank's, and was still caught up in the Sinatra magic. He obviously had a good time, chumming around with Frank, and probably telling a million stories that no one believed. He had arrived in Vegas with all of that still in his mind. Finally – and thankfully – he stopped singing and sat down, and I gave him a drink. He was talking at a pretty fast pace, and I couldn't get him to shut up. He said, "Rich, if you could talk in my voice for 24 hours a day, there's no degree of greatness you could not obtain in the world of show business." I said, "Howard, you're full of BS." "Probably," he said, "but, I'll never tell a lie." I finally had to leave the dressing room to go downstairs to do the show; but even when I was onstage, I could hear, way off in the distance, Howard Cosell singing "New York, New York."

The funniest experience I ever had with Howard was the time the two of us were in Albany, New York. I'd probably been doing a show, and I don't know what Howard was doing there. One morning, we found ourselves at a small airport, just the two of us, waiting for our planes to pick us up and fly us back to New York City. He said, "Rich, I don't know what they're sending for you, but if you like, you could join me on my jet." "Well, that would be nice," I said, "but they'll probably send a prop plane for me, and I can't very well say 'forget it.'" We chatted for a while – Howard was as talkative as usual, talking about everything and nothing at the same time. Then a plane arrived, and Howard gave a little smile, because it was a prop plane. The pilot got out of the plane and walked up to him. "Mr. Cosell? I'm here to fly you back to New York." Howard turned white. He almost had a heart attack. He staggered and gasped, "What?" The pilot repeated, "I'm here to fly you to New York." "You're here to pick me up in a prop plane? You must be mistaken. You're here to pick up Mr. Little, aren't you?" Howard stammered. "No, I'm here to pick you up." Howard exploded. "The gall, the absolute gall of ABC to send a prop plane to fly a man of my stature to New York. This is outrageous! I don't believe it! I'm a superstar! I'm one of the great personalities of the 20th century, and they're picking me up in a *prop plane*! Do you think that Princess Di, do you think that the Queen, do you think that Barbara Streisand or Frank Sinatra would be picked up in a prop plane? There's no way I'm flying in a prop plane. Take the plane back and GET ME A JET!" The pilot stood by and listened to this rant, then he patiently replied, "Sir, I'm not authorized to do that. Besides, by the time I go back and get a jet and fly back here, it will be well into late afternoon." Howard was beside himself. Then my plane arrived. I was praying it would be a jet, but it wasn't. It was just another prop plane, but under the circumstances, I really didn't care. Howard watched my plane pull up, and muttered under his breath, "I think your plane is bigger than mine." I said, "Yeah, I think it is. But it's still a prop plane." He went on, "Rich, I know you've done well in show business, but you're nowhere near the icon that I am." Then he got on the telephone and called Roone Arledge, who was then president of ABC News and Sports. He couldn't get Arledge on the phone, so he subjected one of Arledge's assistants to a tirade about how dare they send him a prop plane! The assistant finally managed to cut in, "We're sorry, Mr. Cosell, but it was all we could come up with on short notice. But it will get you to New York. It's a beautiful afternoon, and you shouldn't have any trouble." That wasn't good enough for Howard. He berated this poor assistant like you wouldn't believe. Then he hung up, turned to me, and continued to rant and rave about the prop plane. Finally, I managed to ask him, "Well, what are you going to do?" He replied, "I'm going to drive to New York. I've got interviews to do later in the day, and I can probably make it. I'll rent a limo. What are you doing?" I said, "I'm going to take the plane they sent for me." "A *prop plane?*" I answered, "It's fine with me. It's not dangerous, y'know. It's got two engines and it's a beautiful day. We won't have any trouble." Well, he just couldn't do it. He stormed out of there and got a limo, and I took my prop plane to New York. Needless to say, I arrived safely. I had a couple of interviews to do on arrival, then *Tom Snyder's Tomorrow* show later in the day. My first interview was around three o'clock, and it went very well. I headed for a second radio interview at another studio in Manhattan. As I walked in, I could hear Howard's voice over the PA, and I realized he was on the air. I heard his voice booming, "Do you *believe* they sent a prop plane for a man of my importance? But they *did*! I still can't believe it! There was a terrible, terrible mistake. I mean, I just don't *fly* in prop planes." He just couldn't let it go, and now he was doing it on the air, live!

Me with Lou Gossett, Jr. & Howard Cosell at my Friar's Roast – New York: 1987

Whenever I saw Howard at various events after that incident, I could never resist the temptation to go up to him and say, "Hi, Howard. Did you fly in by prop plane?" I'd get the dirtiest look, then he'd turn away from me and start singing. But as controversial as he was – and to some people he was a pain in the butt – I found him very amusing and I had a lot of fun doing my impression of him.

Robert Goulet

The Court Jester

Robert Goulet was a great friend of mine. I knew him for over 40 years, though I didn't know him in Canada. Most people assumed I did because they thought he was Canadian, though that's not true. He was born in the States, but spent most of his early life in Canada.

I used to watch him on television when I was a teenager. He was a little older than me. He was in a show called *Showtime* with a gal by the name of Shirley Harmer. I was impressed with him back then. I met him very briefly one time at the CBC (Canadian Broadcasting Company) backstage in the makeup room for a couple minutes. I got to know him pretty well when he came to the United States; which, of course, was after he became a household name when he did *Camelot*, which brought him to the attention of the American public. But he was already a big star in Canada. He had great potential. I used to watch Bob Goulet every week on *Showtime*. And I used to turn the television up to get the full impact of his voice. I remember one week I was watching the show. I didn't know it, but my father was trying to take a nap upstairs. There was Bob singing "Rock-a-Bye Your Baby with a Dixie Melody," the TV was at full volume, when my father yelled down, "Turn that racket down please. Turn that down." And I yelled back up, "It's Robert Goulet, Dad." And he said, "Well then, tell him to sing a ballad!"

I liked Bob because he was a lot like Stewart Granger: opinionated at times, occasionally overbearing, and liked to hold court. But unlike Granger, he had a great sense of humor. He liked to laugh a lot. I like people who are outgoing and larger than life. And Bob was certainly larger than life. He had a silly sense of humor though. He was like a clown, with this magnificent voice. When you'd hear him hit those high notes, he'd just astound you. I'd say my three favorite singers of all time are Frank Sinatra, Bing Crosby and Robert Goulet, although Anthony Newley was another one that impressed me too.

It's a pity that hardly anyone remembers Anthony Newley. He wrote a lot of songs with Leslie Bricusse. He became an incredible entertainer: a child actor, a composer and worked Vegas a lot. I learned a lot from Anthony Newley. I would stand in the wings of the theater when we performed together – Anthony opened for me several times, mostly at the Desert Inn Hotel in Las Vegas. I'd be mesmerized watching him. I learned how to build a show, to save the best for last, to know when to get off, know when to come back on, to put a lot of humor in your show, but at times be dramatic – try and touch your audience. That's what Anthony Newley did.

Me, Bob Goulet & Marty Allen
at Liberace's home: 1997

Robert Goulet could do that too, although Bob's humor, at times, was a little childish. I don't think he ever grew up. He was full of pranks. Sometimes on stage, he would be a little silly. I remember once he was singing a ballad, a very touching song, and he would stop right in the middle of it and say, "You hear about the guy who drank a gallon of Fresca? Well, he snowed in his pants." And then he'd finish the song. The audience would look totally perplexed and think, "Well, I guess that was amusing?" but it would break the mood. Bob would do anything for a laugh. He was charming and I liked being around him a lot.

To give you an idea of how silly Bob could be, one time we were working together at the Sands Hotel in Las Vegas. I was opening for him. I stood in the wings and watched him, as I usually did when a great performer was with me. Bob would go out into the audience. If he wasn't smoking, he would take cigarettes out of people's mouths and throw them on the floor. (You could smoke in the showrooms back then.) He thought that was funny. He would just pull them out of their mouths, throw them on the floor, and all the while, just keep singing. Another habit he had was that he was always punching you. Even if you were at a party or out at a restaurant with him, he'd give you a shot in the arm. "How are you sport?" he'd say, and wallop you. One time he overdid it, and I said, "You just about broke my arm!" "Oh yeah," he chuckled, "can't you take a little fun?" I remember one night, I was standing in the wings watching him, while he went out into the audience throwing cigarettes on the floor and punching people. He went up to this big black man and gave him a shot. They guy stood up. I thought he was going to hit Bob. His look – he shot daggers at him. But then, thankfully, he sat back down. Bob quickly moved away and finished his song. When he ended the show and walked off stage, I was standing there. He said, "Gee, this audience is a little uptight. They couldn't take a little kidding." I said, "What do you mean?" "Well, you know me. I was just having fun out there. And I gave this guy a little jab in the arm and he looked like he was going to kill me. I was just clowning around." I said,

Me & Robert Goulet helping Ginger Rogers put her footprints in the Las Vegas Walk of Fame in front of the Riviera Hotel: 1984

"Do you know who that was, Bob?" "No," he said. "Who?" "That was boxing heavyweight George Foreman!" I replied. He just looked at me, gulped, walked into his dressing room and closed the door. I don't think he ended up doing that anymore. But that's just the way Bob was.

I remember another time when I was Bob's opening act. We were performing at the Diplomat Cabaret Theatre in New York. I would come out and do about half an hour, then he'd come out. I saved my impression of Robert Goulet for last, and then I would finish with "If Ever I Would Leave You." There'd be applause, followed by a little lull, and then Bob would come on. That's what was supposed to happen. So, I go through my whole routine, and finally get to the part where I'm about to start singing. Of course, Bob knew I was going to do this, but, unbeknownst to me and the audience, he was standing at the back of the theatre. He had a microphone and told the sound man to turn it up extra loud. When I announced that I would like to finish with a song from one of the great singers of all time, Robert Goulet, and started to sing, Bob sang and drowned me out completely. He sang the whole song, so I just lip-synced it on stage. I thought, "This is great, because the audience thinks this is me singing!" But, of course, it was really coming from Bob in the back of the theatre. When he hit that powerful note at the end, the audience still had not realized it was actually Bob singing. I took a deep bow and got a standing ovation. Then I went offstage and Bob came out and sang his opening song. He took a bow and the audience applauded. Then he said, "Wasn't that a lot better than Rich Little?" And the audience hollered back, "No!"

Bob Goulet and I were friends for over 40 years, but we did have a falling out once and didn't see each other for a couple of years at the end of his life. But luckily, I did get to see him again before he passed away. I think what happened was, we had the same birthday, November 26th, and we'd always phone each other and wish each other a happy birthday. Once in a while, we would get together to have dinner to celebrate our joint birthdays. Vera Goulet, Bob's wife, then decided to start having a birthday party for Bob every year at either a hotel or a famous restaurant in Las Vegas. I was always invited. But, of course, all the attention was for Bob since it was his party and his friends. Then usually, someone who knew me would announce, "Oh, by the way, it's Rich Little's birthday too." And I'd get a little polite applause. As I said, most there were friends of Bob's. Another year rolled around, and Vera threw another party for Bob. And, of course, my then-wife, Marie, and I were invited. But this time, I got no mention at all. Marie was miffed. "Well, it's your birthday too," she said. "I know," I replied, "but they're all Bob's friends. They don't know it's my birthday. Anyway, I don't really care. It's not important." But she was really upset. Marie said, "I don't think we should see them anymore." It's kind of silly now when I think back on it. But, as it turned out, I actually didn't see Bob for a couple of years, and I missed him. Then one day, just on a whim, I decided to go over to his house and visit him. I left my name at the gate and I phoned him. It was about nine o'clock in the morning. He was up having coffee, and he was delighted to see me. He couldn't have been more charming. It was like we'd never been apart. I spent about three hours with him. We joked a lot. We talked about the past and what he was doing. He told me some corny jokes, and I told him some too. We had a great time. Vera wasn't with us. She was still asleep. When I left, I felt good about our reunion and about seeing Bob again. I was so happy that Bob and I had made up. I really had missed him. It was a wonderful morning. Vera was also happy that we mended fences. She's been a dear friend ever since.

About 5 or 6 months later, Bob passed away. He had lung problems. The doctors didn't catch it early enough. I was devastated, as was everyone that knew him. But I'll tell you, he was a real trouper. He would take a date knowing he was very sick. He had to use oxygen when he was offstage. He'd have it waiting in the wings. He would go out and do a show, come off, get some oxygen, and then go back on stage. He was amazing. His voice was tremendous. And he kept working right until the very end. He was a fighter. Unfortunately, he just couldn't beat his affliction. It's sad to think that Bob's gone.

It's interesting how in show business, people forget about you once you're not around anymore. They forget about what a great singer Bob was. All I have to do is put on one of his records and hear his magnificent voice, and think to myself, "My God, there's no singer living like that today." Most of the music today is what young people are listening to. They don't really care about the past. You have singers such as Robert Goulet, Anthony Newley, and Bing Crosby that are almost totally forgotten. They're the greats. It's a shame, in a way, that the kids today aren't exposed to the recordings of Robert Goulet, because I think they'd be amazed what an incredible voice and talent he was.

Orson Welles

Larger Than Life

I first met Orson Welles live on camera. I was shooting a show in London called *The Kopykats* in the early '70s. The whole show consisted of impressionists impersonating movie stars, television performers, and singers, plus a different guest host each week. This particular week, Orson Welles was the guest host. I was on camera doing a simple routine I'd devised called "Celebrity Sneezes." I'd sneeze "ah-choo" in John Wayne's drawl or in Cary Grant's debonair style, or I'd do Louis Armstrong scat-sneezing, and so forth. I didn't know Orson Welles had just arrived on the set and was watching me as I said, "And here's Orson Welles sneezing." Without hesitation, he walked up behind me, put his hand on my shoulder and said, in that deep, rumbling voice, "Rich, I never sneeze," then walked away. They kept that in the show.

He threw himself into *The Kopykats* completely and did everything he was told. He took direction extremely well. We hit it off from the very beginning. He was fascinated at the number of characters I could do, many of whom had never been done before, and many of whom he knew. We got to know each other quite well. One day when we were shooting a scene, the cue card boy came up to Orson and said, "Mr. Welles, is this okay?" "Is what okay?" he responded. "The cue cards. Can you read them?" "Cue cards? I don't need cue cards!" said Orson. "If you want to write them out, fine. I'll use them as backup, just in case. Maybe other actors use them, but not me. Besides, they're printed way too big." "I can print them smaller," the kid said. "Well, print them smaller, but just don't stand anywhere near the actors, because we don't want the audience to know that I use cue cards. Oh, and by the way, at the top of the first card, write 'Frank Gorshin's cue cards.'" "I can stand way up in the bleachers," said the cue card boy. "That'll be fine. Go up into the bleachers where no one can see you." So the fellow disappeared, rewrote all the cards and got up into the bleachers. A few minutes later, he was calling, "Mr. Welles! Mr. Welles!" Orson said, "What is it now?" "Is it okay if I stand here?" "No, no. Further back! Further back!" Now the letters were so small you couldn't see anything at all from that distance, but the kid kept going right to the very back of the bleachers next to the wall, and held up his tiny cards. By this time, he was about 150 feet away. He yelled, "Mr. Welles, is this alright?" "Perfect. Perfect. Just stay there where no one can see you." Of course, this was absurd, but I guess Orson just wanted the security of knowing that the cue cards were there, even though he couldn't see them. When we shot the scene, I caught a glimpse of this poor kid way at the back of the bleachers where no one could see him, and I started to chuckle.

Guest star Orson Wells & me on "The Kopykats":1972

A couple of years after we did *The Kopykats*, I was in Las Vegas when I got a call from Orson telling me that he was finishing up a movie that he had started shooting in Spain years ago, and he had a perfect role for me. I was thrilled. He told me he'd come to Las Vegas that weekend to discuss it. The weekend came and went, but I never heard from him. A few days later I got a call from him. He was in Los Angeles. "I'll be in Las Vegas in a couple of days. I'm going to drive up." I said, "I thought you were coming up last weekend?" "I was, but the plane I was going to take couldn't accommodate me." I gathered from this that the seats weren't big enough for Orson, because at this point in his life he was gigantic. So now he was going to have to drive up. Another week went by, and still no Orson. Then he called me again to tell me he had to go to Europe, but that he really wanted me to play a role in this movie, which was called *The Other Side of the Wind*. He'd already shot some of it and was going to finish shooting somewhere outside of Phoenix, Arizona. He even gave me a start date. I told him I could only give him three weeks, because I was committed to some club dates. "Oh, don't worry about it," he replied. "We'll finish your stuff in about a week and a half."

By this time, I'd read the script. My role was that of a young director studying under an older director to be played by John Huston. This was very exciting to me – working opposite John Huston and being directed by Orson Welles! Others in the cast were Edmond O'Brien, Susan Strasberg, and Mercedes McCambridge. I was in very good company!

I finally went to Phoenix, and started work on *The Other Side of the Wind*. It was a terrific experience. Orson was very gracious and charming and a great director. He even said he would have cue cards for us if we needed them. (This time they were only a few feet away.) This proved to be a blessing, because Orson would rewrite the script almost every night. So we never really knew what we were going to shoot the next day. We all finally realized that there was no point in learning our lines until we got on the set.

Orson was so huge that he couldn't lie down. He would prop himself up in bed to rewrite the script, and I can still see him sitting there like an elephant. When he was directing, he would sometimes try to show us how to do something, and we'd say, "No, no! Don't get up!" because it would take him about three minutes just to get out of the chair that had been made especially for him. We were terrified he'd have a heart attack. And he never tied the laces on his sneakers – I assume because he couldn't reach down to do it – and I was always afraid he would trip and fall down. Between his enormous size and his cigar smoking, we all worried about his health. With John Huston and Orson puffing away on cigars all day, the air was pretty foul. One day, John and I had a scene together in a tiny bathroom. Orson was squashed into a corner with a handheld camera, and John and I were at the washbasin looking into the mirror. It was really cramped. I was supposed to be quite upset in the scene, and we rehearsed it a few times. Orson squinted through the lens and said, "Looks marvelous, Rich. Your emotions are really showing!" By the time we actually shot the scene, I had tears streaming down my face. He came up to me afterward and said, "Rich, you're a really good actor. The way you can turn on the emotion is incredible! You cried real tears!" I said, "Well, I was really involved in the scene." "This is very good stuff here," said Orson. I never had the heart to tell him that the smoke from his and John's cigars was choking me up and causing my eyes to water. It was like shooting through a dense fog. Orson thought that was acting, and who was I to tell him otherwise?

Orson would do anything for a practical joke. In one scene, I was outside a building tapping on a window. The person inside opened the window and asked who I was and what I wanted. I told him, just as the script demanded. The scene ran about 90 seconds. Then Orson yelled, "Cut! That was fine. Now do it again. But this time, when the guy opens the window and asks, 'Who's there?' you say, 'Walter Cronkite,' and do your lines as Walter Cronkite. Then go into Johnny Carson, and David Brinkley," and he named a few others. I asked, "Why?" "Just do it." "But why those people? It doesn't make sense." "Just do it," he insisted. "Go and work it up." So, I went off to practice the voices and the dialogue, and we did the scene again. The guy opened the window and said, "Who's there?" And I did the dialogue first as Walter Cronkite, then as Johnny Carson, and so on. Eventually, Orson called, "Cut! That's marvelous. Print it!" "But Orson," I said, "this doesn't make any sense at all. Why would I be using those voices?" He said, "Well, they have to dub the film in various languages, and it'll drive them crazy in Spain when they don't know who Walter Cronkite and Johnny Carson are!"

On another occasion, we were shooting a scene at a cocktail party. Everyone was in formal dress, milling around, eating and drinking. Mercedes McCambridge, Susan Strasberg, and I all had dialogue in the scene, and we shot the whole morning and into the afternoon. Toward the end of the day, at the end of a take, Orson didn't call, "Cut," but instead said, "Okay everybody, now look down at your feet in total disgust." We all looked over at him for a moment, not quite understanding what he wanted, but he repeated, "Don't look at me, look down at your feet in total disgust!" So we did. And we started to squirm as if something nasty was crawling up our legs, crying, "Ugh! Blah! Yuck!" Orson yelled, "More, more – keep it going!" and after about 20 seconds of this, he yelled, "Cut! Let's move into the other room for another shot." Everyone else just accepted this as if it were standard operating procedure, but not me. I had to ask Orson, "What was that all about? What were we doing,

Orson?" He said, "Oh, there are midgets running between your legs. I'll put them in afterward in Spain." I was dumbstruck, but all I could say was, "Oh, okay," and wonder what the heck kind of movie this was going to be. Sometimes we'd be in the middle of shooting a scene and he'd yell, "Everyone look up! Midgets on the roof!" We'd all look up in unison, then we'd go on with our dialogue. It's too bad the movie was never released, because I could never figure out how the midgets fit into the movie and why they were running between our feet and on the roof.

We had a scene in a car, driving through the outskirts of Phoenix. John was behind the wheel, I was sitting next to him, and Orson was wedged in the back seat with a handheld camera. Another camera was fastened to my side of the car so that I could reach over and activate it when necessary. John started driving. Orson said, "Action!" and we began our dialogue. Then suddenly, Orson yelled, "Cut!" We had driven up on a lawn and through some hedges, and ended up banging into a garbage can. None of this was in the script. When we finally came to a stop, Orson asked, "What's the problem here?" John said, "Y'know, I never really learned how to drive one of these things. Only driven a few times in my life. I don't even have a license." I thought, "Oh my God. Here I am trying to focus on my lines, trying to look very nonchalant, while John is driving onto lawns and through hedges." Next thing I knew, we were on a one-way street going the wrong way! John slowed the car, swung around, and proceeded to back up, nearly sending us into the canal behind us. We came within about three feet of that canal. With Orson's weight and the weight of the camera, we could have been sucked under in seconds. Finally, when I was able to breathe again, I said, "Wow! That was close!" Orson said, "What are you talking about? Think of the headline: 'Orson Welles, Rich Little, and John Huston sucked under canal outside Phoenix.' You couldn't ask for better billing!" At this point, I took over the driving. It was much safer and far more relaxing, and the scene turned out pretty well.

John and Orson had great respect for one another. They were old friends and had worked together previously. Because I had quite a large role in the film, I was privileged to sit with them at lunchtime. They would discuss other actors. Most of the time, their opinions never differed. They'd either praise someone to the skies or tear them to pieces.

There was no middle ground with these guys. John might say, "You know, I don't think much of James Mason." And Orson would ask, "You don't like him?" John would reply, "No, no, I didn't say that. It's just that I don't think he's that great an actor." Now, I happen to be a big fan of James Mason, so I kept my mouth shut. I just sat there listening to these two run down one of my favorite actors. Orson finally said, "He wasn't too bad in *Odd Man Out.* I thought that was his best." John agreed. "Absolutely, absolutely his best. Yes, yes. That was an exception, and of course, most of the credit has to go to Carol Reed." "Of course, of course," responded Orson. "I don't think James could have pulled it off without such a great director." And on and on they went.

Errol Flynn's name came up quite often. They agreed he wasn't the greatest of actors, but he held a certain fascination for them. Orson asked John, "Do you remember the time you whipped the tar out of Errol Flynn?" John didn't, and Orson reminded him. Apparently, Huston and Flynn were at a party, and they started a big argument. The only way to settle it was to duke it out on their host's front lawn. Huston had boxed when he was younger, and Flynn certainly knew how to land one. Orson reminded Huston that he had whipped the daylights out of Flynn. With his Irish drawl, Huston said to Orson, "Thank you Orson, I appreciate that, but it's not quite true. It was more like a draw. Yes, it was a draw." Orson said, "That's not the way I heard it." John put an end to the argument with, "Well, we both had to be carried home."

One lunch time, while we were quietly eating some cold turkey and salad, John said suddenly, "I never cared for Katharine Hepburn." We all looked up, and Orson said, "What?" "I'm not a big fan of hers," John continued. "I think she's a caricature of herself. She wasn't bad in the early days, but now she's really over the top." Orson said, "My sentiments exactly. I couldn't agree with you more. It's not real anymore. It's an imitation of herself." "That's it," said John. "She needs a director who can tone her down." "Exactly," said Orson. "She's much larger than life, and she's become rather annoying. She's a great talent – don't get me wrong – she was marvelous in *The African Queen,* but that's only because you were directing her, John." "She wanted to play it as Eleanor Roosevelt," said John. Orson said, "What, with the teeth and everything?" "No, no.

Just her attitude," said John. "I told her a little bit of Eleanor wouldn't be bad, but not to exaggerate it too much." These two great men literally spent about an hour going back and forth with this kind of banter. So much for that quiet lunch.

While filming *The Other Side of the Wind,* we had an incident that was right out of a Laurel and Hardy movie. We were shooting some scenes in one of the very upscale residential neighborhoods of Phoenix. As with most movies shooting on location, we were all over the sidewalks with actors, makeup tables, wardrobe people and every kind of equipment, when a patrol car pulled up and a cop got out. He looked just like James Finlayson from the old Laurel and Hardy movies, right down to the bad eye! He wanted to know if we had a permit to shoot in this area. Everyone looked at Orson. Of course, we didn't have a permit, and Orson had no intention of getting one. "Well, officer," he started, "it may look like we're shooting a movie here, but we're not. My name is Huggins, and I'm from Philadelphia. My sister is thinking about buying a house in this area, but she's bedridden at the moment, so I came out here and hired this film crew. We're shooting the various houses in the area that are for sale, and we're going to take the film back to her so she can decide which one she wants to buy." I thought Orson did a great job of putting this more-than-slightly-far-fetched story over; and for one moment, I thought the officer was going to buy it. But then he looked around and saw there were no "For Sale" signs on any of the houses. He looked at Orson somewhat quizzically, at which point, John jumped in. "Let me tell you the truth, officer," said John. The officer replied, "Who are you?" "My name is Edward Huggins," John said. "And my sister happens to be an extremely wealthy woman. We're just shooting all the houses in this area so she can pick out one or two that she really likes, and then we'll find out who the owners are and see if they want to sell." Everyone was fixated on the officer, waiting to see if he would buy this story. He thought for a moment, then said, "So you went to all this trouble, hired all these people, with lights, crew, and costumes, just to shoot some houses to show to your wealthy sister?" John and Orson nodded simultaneously. "Yes, officer. This is the true story, sir." "I've never heard such a load of baloney in my life! Get in the squad car. We're going down to the station." I never did find out what the outcome was. I think they were fined, but we never went back to that location!

One afternoon, the three of us found ourselves eating lunch at a Denny's just outside of Phoenix. John and I sat on either side of the table, but Orson couldn't fit at the table, so we found a chair for him to sit in the aisle. No one recognized these two giants of the cinema, but about halfway through lunch, a woman recognized me from *The Ed Sullivan Show*. She was obviously not a movie fan, because she completely ignored John and Orson while lavishing praise on my work and asking for my autograph. So I wrote her a little note, and signed it: "To Martha, Best, Rich Little." She was very pleased, but she kept looking over at John, puffing away at his cigar, and Orson spilling out of the chair in the aisle. When I handed her the autograph, she leaned over, and in a stage whisper asked me, "Who's your fat friend?" I nearly choked on my sandwich. John, without a moment's hesitation, said, "We haven't the foggiest idea. We found the poor devil out on the highway. He looked undernourished, so we brought him in here for fries and a cherry Coke. We're going to fatten him up and send him on his way." Orson said, "Oh, thank you, kind sir. You are very, very hospitable. I do so appreciate your generosity. I thank you most humbly." As for me, I'll never forget the look on that woman's face!

Another day, we were shooting in a house Orson had borrowed from some friends who were in Europe. He told them he wanted to have a quiet place for the summer to write his memoirs. As soon as they left, he moved in all of the equipment and all of the actors; took out walls, rearranged the rooms, made huge cracks in the swimming pool, and generally made a complete mess of their place. Every morning, he would climb onto the roof to check the light with his viewfinder. One day, John and I were told that our call time the next morning would be 4:30, because Orson wanted to shoot a scene on the roof at exactly 5:22 a.m. when the light would be absolutely perfect for that particular scene. We were ready and made up in plenty of time, and we had to rehearse the scene in order for him to get the 40 seconds of very specific light he wanted. It was so dark when we got up on the roof that they had to put lights on us. At precisely 5:22, they cut the lights. Unfortunately, by then, there were problems with the dialogue, problems with the makeup, problems with the costumes, problems all over the place. We finally shot the scene on the roof at quarter to eleven! When it was all over, I asked Orson why he made us get up in the middle of the night to shoot a scene at a quarter to eleven in the morning. He said, "Well, we had to get a lot of practice in. We may have had a lot of problems, but at a quarter to eleven, the light was absolutely perfect for the shot I wanted." Go figure!

Orson was a great listener. He had incredible concentration. He loved stories about show business, and he was a great practical joker. He also had a big heart. Yes, he was an eccentric, but he was always interesting, and he was never cruel. He listened to anyone who had an idea, but he made it clear that he lived in his own world, and you never knew what he was going to do next. You just had to wait and see.

Howard Keel

The Macho Baritone

*W*hen I was about 13 years old, the whole family went to see a musical called *Show Boat* at the Capitol Theater in Ottawa. I'd only seen one musical before – don't remember what it was, but I remember telling my father I thought musicals were stupid. "Why?" he asked. "Well," I said, "they start singing and suddenly there's an orchestra playing. Where's the orchestra? We never see the orchestra." Dad said, "There isn't an orchestra in the movie. The orchestra's put in later." That made no sense to me. "Yeah, but we can hear it. Are they hiding somewhere? Are they behind the bushes or in another room?" My dad had a hard time trying to explain it to me because he was laughing so hard. Anyway, mum and dad dragged the whole family to see Howard Keel and Kathryn Grayson in *Show Boat*. And I loved it! Everything about it was terrific: the music, the acting, the scenery, the costumes, and most of all, the story. It was heart-lifting, it was sad, it was funny – it was a perfect movie. While I was raving about the movie in the car on the way home, I asked my dad who had played the leading man. He said, "That was Howard Keel, a man's man." If I ever met him, I would like to shake his hand and tell him how good he was in *Show Boat*." My brothers looked at each other and sniggered, "Yeah. Sure, Dad, when are you going to Hollywood?" and we all kind of smiled. Wouldn't you know, over 20 years later, I actually met Howard Keel. I walked up to him and shook his hand. I said, "This is for my father. You were great in *Show Boat*." He was startled. "Oh …well…thank you very much!" He knew who I was and he asked, "Was that one of your favorites?" I said, "Absolutely! When I saw it with my family back in 1951, my father wanted to shake your hand and tell you how great you were in that movie. Well, it took me over 20 years, but I've done it."

I met Howard Keel at the home of a fellow named Norman Sedawie who produced and directed some of my shows. In fact, it was Norman who directed the variety show in Toronto where Mel Tormé and I worked together for the first time. Norm was producing a stage version of *Seven Brides for Seven Brothers*, and he'd asked the whole cast over to his home. I was invited too, so that's how I came to meet Howard. We didn't see each other again for many, many years, which was my loss. But when we did meet again eventually, we became pretty close friends during the last five years of his life. I thought he was one of the most fascinating, interesting, nicest people I'd met in the business. He was a bit like my other good friend, Stewart Granger, but not as brash and outspoken, and certainly not as self-centered. Keel was a no-nonsense guy, a big man with a big voice, and very, very handsome. In fact, like Granger, he got better looking as he got older.

One evening, we all went out to dinner together: Howard Keel, Stewart Granger, me, and my then-wife, Jeanne. We had a nice meal somewhere in Malibu, and I remember Granger saying to Howard, "Howard, you were at MGM the same time I was. You started there about 1950. So did I. And we both met a lot of people. Who did you *not* like at MGM? Who did you not admire, and who were you not too crazy about?" Howard paused for a moment, and then said, "Well, Stewart, to tell you the honest truth, I wasn't too crazy about you." Howard didn't pull any punches. I held my breath, and looked at Granger's face. For a moment he said nothing. Then he gave a little smile and said, "Pass the peas, please."

Me & Howard Keel

Howard Keel was the epitome of a great movie star. He could do musicals, dramas, comedies – you name it. I've always thought he should have been a bigger star than he was, although he was pretty big in the '50s. Besides *Show Boat*, he did several MGM movie musicals, among them: *Annie Get Your Gun, Seven Brides for Seven Brothers, Kiss Me Kate,* and *Rose Marie.* He also starred in a few dramatic movies:

Desperate Search, Floods of Fear, and *War Wagons.* The problem is, you get type-cast in this business. I know this. I've auditioned for many roles in my career and the producer or director has said, "But you're an impersonator. How do we know you can act?" Howard Keel was labeled as a musical comedy actor, and if MGM wasn't planning to do a movie musical that had a potential role for him, he just waited. Once in a while, he did something else. But I think he should have been given more dramatic roles while at MGM. He did, however, get to play more varied roles in the theater. He was marvelous in *Plaza Suite* and *Sunrise at Campobello.* I really thought that after *Show Boat,* he'd be as big as Clark Gable, or that he'd end up like Frank Sinatra, playing in musicals, drama, and comedy roles. He did, but not enough.

What really drew me to Howard Keel, was that he was a great storyteller. He was full of fascinating anecdotes about movies I'd loved in the past. He had a gentle nature, but he could be quite feisty at times. During the filming of *War Wagons,* John Wayne started picking on him. Wayne was a pretty good guy, but toward the end of his life, his health was not good, and he knew he was living on borrowed time. And as such, he often became irritable. One day, Howard took him aside and said, "Listen, I feel sorry for you. I know you've only got one lung. Well, I've got two lungs, and I'm an inch taller than you, so if you get out of line with me one more time, I'm going to put you on your ass." They got along fine after that.

One summer, I went down to Palm Springs to see Howard. He was starring in *The Palm Springs Follies,* which featured older dancers and singers, many of whom had retired to that part of California where people move to benefit from the beautiful climate and easy living. Howard was the guest star that summer, and he was great, as usual. His voice was not what it once was, but he could still belt it out. I asked the manager if I could go backstage to see Howard after the show, but he wouldn't let me. He told me that after the show, all the stars would put on gloves and go out in the lobby for 20 minutes to pose for pictures and sign autographs. "Put on gloves?" I asked. "Yes, the cast puts on white gloves, because they shake a lot of hands, and this protects them from germs." I must admit, I found that quite unusual, but sensible. I never do that, but

I always wash my hands later in the dressing room. I found Howard out front, meeting and greeting folks, but he was only wearing one glove. I asked him why. He said, "I'm doing my Michael Jackson impression." And, he proceeded to do Michael Jackson's "moonwalk" across the lobby of the theater. It wasn't great, but it was better than I could have done! Everyone applauded and Howard took a bow. Then, he put on the other glove, and I asked him, "Who are you going to do now? Jolson?" And with that, he got down on one knee and started to sing "Mammy." More applause. I said, "That was really good." "Yeah!" he exclaimed. "I should put on a show and take out 'Ol' Man River' and do 'Swanee' instead. It would get a better reaction."

My late wife Marie and I had a great rapport with Howard and his wife, Judy. The four of us often had dinner together. Howard and I played the same game I used to play with Sinatra: "fill in the blanks." Howard would try to remember the name of some movie or some director, and I'd immediately come up with it. "How did you know that?" he'd say. "You weren't even there!" "I know, but I read a lot," I replied. He had a wonderful sense of humor, and he was a workaholic. He may not have gotten all the roles he really wanted, but that didn't stop him from working. When he wasn't making a film, he'd be traveling all over the world taking whatever was offered to him. He and Judy loved to travel, and he loved to work.

Whenever I mention Howard Keel or Stewart Granger to young people today, they always say to me, "Who?" It's too bad they don't take a look at their films. Just because the films are old, or in black and white, and don't have millions of dollars' worth of special effects, doesn't mean they weren't any good. Too many younger people today are only interested in what's happening in the here and now. They could learn so much if they'd just visit the past once in a while. When I was a kid, I was fascinated with the past. I still am. I live in the present, but history has always been a big draw for me, especially as it related to the world of entertainment. I'd sit on the stairs and listen to the grownups talk all evening. My dad would say, "I'll allow you to sit there, but only if you don't say a word, and don't let anyone know you're there." I'd spend two or three hours like that, just sitting on the stairs listening to them talk. Can you imagine kids doing that today? They'd be bored out of their minds. Today, you're lucky if you get a "hello" or "goodbye" out of them. Kids tend to be more into their own thing these days. They're not very interested in what older people are doing. Older people – you know, people 30, 35, 40.

Howard Keel was a giant, whether generations X & Y know it or not. I miss him, and it was an absolute pleasure to know him – even if it was for only a few years.

John Wayne

Everyone's Hero

*J*ohn Wayne (The Duke) was larger than life. When I was a kid, I admired Jimmy Stewart and Gregory Peck and Burt Lancaster; but John Wayne was a super-hero, the kind of guy all kids wanted to emulate: tough, macho, heroic, and with a bit of an edge. I met him three times and he was always extremely kind to me. Maybe it was because I impersonated him, and that intimidated him a bit, or maybe it was just because I caught him in a good mood. In any event, he seemed to get quite a kick out of my impression of him. I heard that John Wayne could be ornery and sarcastic, and tough on people he didn't take to, but he seemed to warm up every time he saw me.

The first time I met him was in the '70s when I was doing a variety show for NBC. One day, there was some buzz that John Wayne was on the lot doing a cameo for the television show *Rowan & Martin's Laugh-In* on Stage 5. Of course, I'd admired the man all my life and had imitated him since I was 18 years old, so I was determined to get a look at him in person. I wandered over to Stage 5 during a rehearsal break. I had no problem getting on the set, but there was a mass of people hanging around, all trying to get a glimpse of John Wayne. I realized I might never get to meet him, but I stood around for 10 or 15 minutes, even though I couldn't see the action too well from my vantage point. Then, a passing grip told me they were pressed for time. Wayne had to get through his *Laugh-In* spots by six o'clock, because he had a plane to catch. By this time, it was about twenty till six, so I knew it would be impossible for me to meet him. But I thought I'd just hang around until he finished anyway. Just as I was about to leave, I heard a loud voice say, "Hold it there, mister! Rich Little, get over here on the double!" Well, I'd heard that voice so many times in the movies that I stiffened up and was back over there like a shot. How he picked me out of the crowd, how he could see me leaving, I had no idea. The next thing I knew, I was standing right in front of him, and the whole crowd was watching us. He looked me up and down and said, "They tell me you do me better than I do, and you do my walk pretty good too. Show me how I do it. I'm losin' it." This got a big laugh from everyone around, including Rowan and Martin. I said, "Are you joking?" Duke said, "No, show me how I do my walk. I've heard you do the voice, but never seen you do the walk. I gotta get outta here soon, so let's see it." I looked around, deeply embarrassed, and thought, "Can I pull this off right in front of the man himself?" I tried to pull myself together as best I could, because when John Wayne ordered you to do something, you pretty well jumped to it, just as Harry Carey did in *She Wore a Yellow Ribbon* or John Agar did in *The Sands of Iwo Jima*. When Sgt. Stryker spoke, you'd better do what he told you! He said, "All right, everybody move back and give the kid some room." Now I had no choice. I had to do something fast. So I started into the John Wayne walk, and I ambled across the set. Under the circumstances, I thought I had done a pretty good John Wayne. When I finished, everybody applauded, including Wayne. Then he looked me right in the eye, put his hands on his hips, and said, "So that's how I do it. Hell, I've been walking like Loretta Young all these years, and didn't even know it! What do you do with me in your act?" I told him, "I've done a lot of things over the years, but right now I'm doing a little scene from *The Sands of Iwo Jima.*" "Let's hear it!" "Now??" The *Laugh-In* crew and various members of his entourage started to check their watches, but he didn't seem at all concerned. He just wanted to hear what I did in my act. So once again, I got my courage up, and I said, "All right, listen, and listen tight! At ease, men. Tomorrow we're gonna hit the beaches of Iwo Jima again. It's gonna be murder out there. Some of ya ain't gonna be comin' back. Wish like hell I could be goin' with ya, but I picked up a nasty cold." Well, that got a huge laugh. Wayne grinned, "That's funny. Did you write that?" I said, "No, I think I took it from the *Sands of Iwo Jima.*" "You probably did. And I'll bet you get a great reaction! What else do you do?" Now his people were trying to get him out of there, but he kept saying, "Yeah, yeah, yeah ..." Then he turned to me and said, "Keep up the good work. You know something? I don't think I need a PR man anymore – you're doin' it for me." I said, "It's a pleasure to meet you. It really is. I'm so sorry I took up so much of your time." "No problem. I've been dyin' to see that walk! Pat [his son] said he'd seen you do it on *The Tonight Show* and told me I had to take a look at it." I said goodbye, and as I walked away doing the John Wayne walk, he called over to me, "Hey, don't get it down too good, or you'll get yourself arrested." That was such a big moment for me, that I had a hard time getting back to work.

John Wayne, Jimmy Stewart & me at the Variety Club tribute to Jimmy: 1978

I met Duke again a couple of times, once at some crowded celebrity function where I didn't have a chance to say too much to him, and the last time was at a tribute to Jimmy Stewart at which I was performing. I got the chance to chat for a while with Jimmy, Glenn Ford, and Duke. As always, I felt very honored to be in the presence of such great men, all of whom I imitated.

But I couldn't resist one temptation: whenever one of them asked me a question, I'd respond in their voice. They all got quite a kick out of this, then Jimmy beckoned to a friend of his, someone I didn't know. He turned to me and said, "Can you do him?" "I don't even know who he is!" The Duke said, "That surprises me. I thought you did everybody!"

I think that in life you should only form opinions about people by the way they treat you, and that you shouldn't listen to what other people say, or believe what you read. You should form your own opinion by the way someone interacts with you. I'm happy to report that I can only say good things about John Wayne.

Paul Lynde

A Sad Comedian

*P*aul Lynde was one of the funniest men I've ever known in my life. He could get a laugh by simply reading from the phone book. He had funny material, he was funny to look at, and had a funny delivery. And, because he was gay, he was completely over the top. Early in his career, most people didn't know he was gay. It wasn't something talked about in those days, and people thought it was part of his act. Later on, of course, it became more accepted, and he used a lot of thinly-veiled gay humor on television. I got great mileage out of doing Paul Lynde over the years. In fact, I still do, because so many people still remember him. He was primarily responsible for the huge success of *Hollywood Squares* and was immensely popular as Uncle Arthur on *Bewitched*. He had a few shots at a show of his own, but none of them succeeded. Like Tim Conway, he was a great second banana. I think this bothered him. He was a very troubled man, very moody, and not terribly friendly. But that didn't stop him from being one of the funniest men of his generation.

I did a lot of *Hollywood Squares* in the '70s, and I've always felt that the first version, the one with Charley Weaver, George Gobel, Rose Marie, Wally Cox, and all those wonderful people was the best version of the show. Charley Weaver (Cliff Arquette) was down in the left-hand corner, and when Cliff passed away, George Gobel took that spot. During filming, I sometimes laughed so hard, I had tears streaming down my face. In fact, to be honest with you, I occasionally wet myself. Sitting right under me on *Hollywood Squares* was…oh, I can't remember – I think he drowned. Oh, now I remember, it was Pee Wee Herman.

Whenever I did Paul on *Hollywood Squares*, the camera would immediately cut to him for a reaction, but there usually wasn't one. He'd make a face and say, "Who's he doing? Who is that? Does that sound like me?" It was all a put-on. He knew. But I always felt he wasn't happy when I impersonated him. He once saw my brother Fred do him on some show, and told everybody that my brother did him better than I did. Maybe he did.

I think he never warmed up to me because I imitated him. Perhaps it was due to the fact that I exaggerated him slightly and made
him look a little more effeminate. Still, I found him very interesting. He
was very bright and was a great conversationalist. But, he drank heavily. We'd tape five episodes of *Hollywood Squares* at a time, usually on a
weekend, starting at four o'clock in the afternoon. We'd have dinner
after the third show, then shoot two more. By the time we finished dinner, Paul was pretty well out of it. I used to fear that he'd fall out of his
square! Of course, he was even funnier when he was drunk. He'd look
really sour, and then he'd come out with a line that was so funny it
would just kill you. But liquor was his crutch and his downfall. I'll
never know how some of the things he said got on the air. He once

came out with a one-liner that just destroyed everyone on the show. In fact, I think a couple of people actually did fall out of their squares! Peter Marshall asked Paul a cooking question: "In preparing chicken tetrazzini, you should always remove something from the chicken first. What is it?" Without a moment's hesitation, Paul said, "The rooster." Well, we had to stop taping. It took about five minutes for the audience to recover. It wasn't just *what* he said, it was *how* he said it. "Paul, can you circumcise a whale?" "Yes, but you're going to need *fore* skin divers." One time I was chatting with Paul at a party, when we heard a huge crash in the kitchen. Without batting an eye, Paul said, "Uh-oh. I knew she was trouble."

Glen Campbell used to tell a story about performing at the Hilton Hotel in Las Vegas. He'd open the show with one of his popular numbers, then he'd bring his brother out, and the two of them would sing. Then he'd bring out his parents, and all four of them would sing. One night, Glen saw Paul sitting in the front row, and he introduced him, "Ladies and gentlemen, from *Hollywood Squares*, Mr. Paul Lynde. Paul, take a bow." Paul stood up and the place erupted. When the applause died down, Glen leaned over and said to Paul, "Gosh Paul, you're so popular! Did you ever think of doing a nightclub act like I'm doing?" Paul said, "I can't. My parents are dead."

Paul would also come to the Sands Hotel to see me perform. He'd sit in the front row and was always half in the bag. If I paused for a moment, he'd yell out, "Do Godzilla!" At first I'd ignore him, but then it became annoying. I'd say, "And now I'd like to do my Richard Nixon impression…" and that voice would cry out, "No! We want to hear Godzilla!"

Another classic story that went around Hollywood for a while was so outrageous, that it had to be true. One night, Paul was driving home from a taping of *Hollywood Squares*, feeling no pain, weaving all over the highway. A motorcycle cop pulled him over to the side of the road, sauntered over to Paul's car, rapped on the glass, and Paul rolled down the window. The cop took out a pad and pencil, and Paul said, "I'll have a Big Mac, an order of fries, and a Cherry Coke," and then drove away. Apparently, the cop thought it was so funny that he didn't pursue him, so Paul got away with it. His humor got him out of many scrapes.

I think Paul got tired of doing *Hollywood Squares*. He did it for so many years, and he made a lot of dough out of it. But he wasn't very successful in other areas of television, even though his recognition factor was incredible. Near the end, there wasn't much energy or enthusiasm. Once in a while, he'd come out with a great line, but it was sad to see his decline. It's too bad that such a talented man disintegrated so quickly. Like many entertainers in Hollywood, he probably couldn't take the pressure of success. I've often wondered that if talented people such as Paul or Elvis Presley or Marilyn Monroe had never become stars, they might have enjoyed simple, happy lives and lived to be 85 years of age. Maybe. But maybe not.

Johnny Carson

King of Late Night

*J*ohnny Carson was a hard man to get to know. I never really knew him. I'm not sure whether even his wives knew him. I appeared on *The Tonight Show* many, many times and hosted it on about 12 of those occasions. That show did a tremendous amount of good for my career. However, just about all of the time I spent with Johnny was on *The Tonight Show* stage. I never visited him in his dressing room, either before or after the show, and he never visited me in mine. We'd sometimes talk during the commercial breaks, but mostly about what was scheduled on the show. I'd see him drive up in his little Mercedes and park in his special parking spot right in front of the entrance. Sometimes we'd exchange pleasantries when we left the building, then he'd climb back into his little car and drive away. He was one of the few celebrities who drove his own car, and I often wondered if he ever caused any accidents when people looked over and recognized him. There were no airs about Johnny Carson. He was a pretty nice guy, but he was a loner and liked to keep to himself. He had very few close friends, so I never saw him on the social circuit. Once in a while, I'd run into him at a restaurant or in a store in Malibu, and we'd talk for a minute or two.

Me & Johnny Carson on "The Tonight Show": 1982

What made Johnny Carson great was that he was a great listener. He could bounce off what people were talking about. Many hosts, including yours truly, can get a bit nervous and will constantly look down at the next question on the card in front of them. If you're not focused on what the guest is saying, you can get into real trouble. For example, the guest could be talking about someone he murdered, and you come back with, "So, what's new and exciting?" The key is to always have the next question in your mind, or just glance at the card quickly, but you must be able to play off what the guest is talking about at that moment so you can keep the momentum going and not suddenly change the subject. Johnny was a master of this technique. He always had his notes there, but he rarely referred to them. He had the amazing ability to come back with exactly the right question, always adding a bit of humor if the guest was a bit boring, so that he could turn the dreariest guests into fascinating and funny interviews. He knew how to make the guest look good; and he'd let them talk, as long as they had something interesting to say. He'd never butt in, or try to make himself look good at the guest's expense. He would only override a guest when he really had to. And his wonderful, all-American, boy-next-door quality put everyone at ease.

I had a falling out with *The Tonight Show* in the early '80s, although to this day, I don't really understand what happened. All I know is that after numerous appearances on the show, both as a guest and as a guest host, they stopped asking me. It just suddenly came to an end. I thought perhaps I'd said something to offend Johnny, or maybe Freddie DeCordova, the producer, or Bobby Quinn, the director. Who knows? Suddenly I was a "no-book." I went down to *The Tonight Show* several times over the years, trying to find out what had happened, but all I got was, "Oh, Rich. You're the best impersonator. We think you're great. But we're just not booking impersonators anymore. If we do, you'll be the first one we call." I always felt this was kind of a cop-out. I would have preferred them to be more straight-forward and tell me to my face what the problem was, rather than getting this runaround. It was particularly galling that Johnny later hired other impressionists on a couple of his anniversary shows. Over the years, I've heard several stories as to why I suddenly became a pariah on *The Tonight Show*. There was a rumor that I'd said something bad about Bobby Quinn, the show's director, but I can't imagine I did. I never threw my weight around when I hosted the show. It's not my nature, and besides, I was too scared to try that! Frankly, hosting *The Tonight Show* was a huge responsibility, and I would shake most of the time. It was a "live" show, in that it was live on tape; meaning that you went from beginning to end without a break, and without being able to reshoot anything. I relied very heavily on

Freddie DeCordova to guide me through, and he was always a tremendous help. Another theory was that my jokes about Johnny rubbed him the wrong way, even though I'd been doing my impression of him on his own show for years. Or maybe something was taken out of context and reported back to him the wrong way. Someone pointed out that my appearances on *The Tonight Show* dried up after Reagan took office. Johnny liked to do his own impression of the president (and did so very well, too), but I doubt this was the reason. I must admit that I was more than a bit sad that almost everyone who ever appeared on *The Tonight Show* was invited back during his final year to say one last goodbye, but I was not included in that group. I would like to have had an opportunity to thank him one last time, in his own arena, for everything he did for my career.

Johnny Carson & me at an award ceremony for Vice President Hubert Humphrey

The last time I saw Johnny Carson was after he retired. He was in a restaurant in Malibu, sitting in a booth next to me. He came over, which surprised me. He said, "Rich, you're still performing aren't you?" I said, "Yeah, all around the country." "I guess you don't do me in your act anymore," he replied. "Of course I do!" I responded. "It's one of my most popular impressions." "But I haven't been on TV in years. Do they still remember me?" I told him, "Johnny, people will always remember you. You're a legend." "You're kidding?" he said. "You're really still doing me?" "Of course," I replied. "Well, thanks for keeping me alive." Little did I know he would live only a few more years. He went back to his table, but I don't think he believed what I said. It goes to show you how insecure entertainers are.

I couldn't say it then, so I'll say it now: "Thanks, Johnny. You will always be my most popular impression."

Frank Sinatra

Chairman of the Board

*W*hy was a man as successful and beloved as Frank Sinatra so angry, so moody? He could sit in a dark room for hours brooding. He could lash out at any time. He could be ruthless, cruel, and a bully. Then, at other times, he was a pussycat – fun-loving, caring, charming, and great to be around. Fortunately, the latter was the Frank Sinatra I knew. When he was in a good mood, he was my kind of guy. But he was a time-bomb set to explode. His mood could change in seconds. He was a success in almost everything he did: movies, records, stage, television, radio. The one exception was golf. I once saw him tee off and was tempted to call the National Guard! I don't know why he didn't just move the hole closer to the tee. But when he set his mind to it, he could be the best. Like so many of the celebrities I've known, Frank loved to talk about the past – the people he'd known, the movies he'd made. Frank would often hold court. I've read many biographies, and I've always been interested in "Old Hollywood," so most of the time, I knew what he was talking about. Occasionally, I'd throw in an anecdote or a funny line. This he liked. As long as you weren't trying to impress him, bullshit him, or overshadow him, you were considered a friend. He liked people who could make him laugh – Don Rickles, Charlie Callas, Foster Brooks, and Red Buttons, to name a few.

I think the first time I met Frank was at a benefit I did in Palm Springs, back in the mid '70s, for the Betty Ford Clinic. I was doing a routine of various presidents, saying funny, stupid things. I saved Gerald Ford for last, because he was the guest of honor at this benefit. Well, they introduced me, and when I came on, I immediately saw that Gerald Ford was sitting right in front of me; Frank Sinatra at his side. It was a very high stage, and they were down about three feet, in the first row. I thought, "Well, I'd better be pretty good with those two sitting there." So, I went through my presidents. I forget exactly who I did – I'm sure Nixon was in there – but when I got to Gerald Ford, I overdid him a little bit, because he was sitting right in front of me and I wanted to impress him. The Ford routine consisted of me walking up to the podium, tripping and falling right into it, which then broke into a million pieces. Although it looked like wood, it was, in fact, made of cork. When I hit the podium, I was supposed to fall down on the floor. I'd done this on many club dates, and it brought the house down, as well as me. I overdid it a little bit. I hit the podium. It flew into a million pieces. I lost my balance, fell off the stage, and landed in Gerald Ford's lap! We were both covered in cork, and Frank was falling off his chair, pounding the floor, tears of laughter streaming down his face. I'd had the presence of mind to grab the microphone as I fell, and put it up to Gerald Ford's mouth. His comment was, "Whoops!" At first I thought I'd killed the President of the United States as I landed on him. I wasn't sure if I'd hurt him or not, but when he said, "Whoops!" I knew everything was okay. This was the beginning of my relationship with Frank. And from that point on, for the next five years or so, I was considered a friend. He thought I was one of the funniest people he'd seen in his life. Anyone who could make Frank Sinatra laugh to that degree was considered an insider. It was an incredible moment for me; and, I guess, an incredible moment for Gerald Ford. Vinnie Falcone, Frank's conductor and dear friend of mine, was there too. He said Frank talked about this for years.

Me with President Gerald Ford

I remember when I left that evening, we were waiting for our cars to be brought around, and I shook hands with Gerald Ford. He was still laughing, and I happened to notice that he still had cork in his hair!

I did a lot of charity work with Frank in the '70s — benefits in Palm Springs, San Francisco, and New York. One time, I did a benefit with Frank and Ella Fitzgerald — I think it was at Carnegie Hall in New

York – and my rehearsal was in the afternoon. I'd been told that Frank hardly ever came to rehearsal, so I wasn't expecting to see him. I was rehearsing with the orchestra, running through a lot of my singing impressions: Tony Bennett, Perry Como, Kenny Rogers, Tom Jones – and then I did "My Kind of Town," Frank's big number from *Robin and the Seven Hoods*. I went through some of his mannerisms as I sang, but what I didn't know, was that he was watching me from the back of the stage. If I'd known, I probably would have seized up and my impression of him would have sounded like Porky Pig. Anyway, I was about half way through the song when he snuck up behind me and started to sing along with me. All of a sudden, there were two Frank Sinatras singing. As I did some of his mannerisms, he'd say, "No, I don't do it like that. I do *this* and then I do *this*, and then I stamp my foot *here*." Obviously, I was thrilled; and that night, when I did the show, I put in all the things he'd told me to do. When the show was over, he said, "Hey, kid, you do a pretty good Frank Sinatra!" Then he stamped his foot.

In the early part of his career, Frank threw his weight around a lot. He was in a slump before *From Here to Eternity*, but that film made his career take off again like a skyrocket. He was very impatient and he didn't like to rehearse or do two takes of anything, much like his friend Dean Martin. He was a man in a hurry. He hated incompetence. If you made a mistake, he'd say, "That's your problem, not mine. You fix it." Of course, when he was around the people he liked, when his career was going great, or when a movie he was in was a success, he was probably one of the nicest people in show business. But as I mentioned, that mood could change at the drop of a hat.

I only saw something even remotely resembling the angry side of Frank Sinatra on one occasion. I was visiting his compound in Palm Springs. My then-wife, Jeanne, and I were his guests for the weekend. He couldn't have been more gracious. He did most of the cooking. He'd spend hours making spaghetti sauce. He was always very polite and gracious to women. "Can I get you anything?" "Is there anything you need?" "Are you comfortable?" On Sunday morning, I noticed two guys working in his den, trying to balance a pool table. I guess the pool table was a new acquisition. As you may know, a pool table must be perfectly

Frank Sinatra & me

level. This was a big job, and these guys were working away feverously, screwing the legs up and down, measuring and calculating. They literally spent hours trying to get it absolutely perfect. They finally left at about four o'clock. Then around 5:30 or 6:00, one of the butlers came in with a rollaway cart laden with drinks and hors d'oeuvres: chips, peanuts, assorted things like that. Right next to the newly installed pool table was a very heavy lamp, set in marble. The butler couldn't get the cart past these two pieces of furniture. So, rather than trying to move the lamp, he simply shoved the pool table as far as he could – about two or three feet – to get the rollaway cart through. Well, Frank walked in just as the butler had finished pushing the pool table and stood there with his mouth open. I thought, "Oh boy, this is going to be interesting." Frank just stood there dumbfounded – he couldn't get the words out. He was stuttering. I guess the butler was not a very bright man, but Frank must have liked him. Fortunately, after a moment, Frank just started to roar with laughter, and what started out as a potential disaster for the butler, turned into a huge joke. How anyone, *anyone*, could have moved the pool table instead of the lamp was just beyond him. He laughed so hard, that we all started laughing – even the poor butler. But this was one time when Frank's anger turned to laughter. It didn't happen very often.

That same weekend, I mentioned a charity event to Frank that I was going to do in my hometown of Ottawa, Canada. I was raising money for the Ottawa Civic Hospital to build a neo-natal center. It was going to cost

THANKS FRANK!

For coming to my hometown of Ottawa and performing with me on September 11th. For helping raise one million dollars for Ottawa Civic Hospital. And mostly, for being my friend.

With deep appreciation,

Rich

Frank Sinatra & me at the Ottawa Civic Hospital Benefit: 1982

at least a million dollars. I'd been trying to put together a show with Paul Anka and me, because we both came from Ottawa, and we were both lucky enough to have hit it big. But I could never pin Paul down. Every time my manager contacted him, he got, "Well, we'll let you know." This went on month after month – he just wouldn't commit. When I mentioned this to Frank, he said, "Forget Paul Anka. I'll do it." I said, "What?" "I'll do it. What's the date?" I gave him a tentative date when we hoped to do the show, about eight months away. He wrote it down in his "Miss Piggy" calendar – I wonder if Miss Piggy knew he was a big fan of hers! "Just give me the date, the time, and the place, and I'll bring the whole orchestra up by plane from New York. It won't cost anyone a penny. You've done a lot of dates for me. It's time to pay you back." "This is absolutely fantastic," I thought. Sure enough, he did it. He flew up to Ottawa with the entire orchestra in a private plane, landed at the airport at about six o'clock, and got to the auditorium at around twenty to seven. I'll tell you, a lot of people, including yours truly, were pretty relieved to see him, because the only confirmation I'd had from him was, "I'll be there." He could have gotten lost, he could have had the date wrong, the weather could have been bad, he could have had engine trouble – any number of things could have prevented him from showing up. My good friend, Gord Atkinson, was involved with this benefit, and he was really concerned that Frank might not make it. Quite a few well-to-do people had paid a lot of money to have dinner with Frank Sinatra and see the show. Well, Frank didn't really make it to the dinner, but he did make it in time for dessert, in time to shake a few hands and have a few pictures taken. It worked out just fine. However, I do remember Gord coming to me in a state of panic, and saying, "Rich, how good is your

Frank Sinatra?" "What do you mean?" "I mean, if he doesn't show up, we could be run out of town. I could bring the lights way down and you could pretend you're Frank." I said, "Funny…very funny." The show was a tremendous success. Frank was the opening act. He was extraordinarily gracious in letting me be the headliner and close the show. He said, "It's your hometown. *You* should be the headliner." He did have an ulterior motive though. He wanted to do his 30 or 40 minutes and get back on the plane to New York before the bars closed. So, the second he was through, he was out of there – gone! The Prime Minister of Canada, Pierre Elliot Trudeau, was at the show. Even while Frank was on, he kept asking my wife, Jeanne, what kind of a guy he was, and all sorts of questions – "What does he eat?" "Who are his friends?" "Does he listen to his own music?" He was obviously a big fan. Doing that show with Frank Sinatra for the Civic Hospital was one of the highlights of my career. And, the Rich Little Special Care Nursery is still going strong today.

Back in the '70s, I was appearing at the MGM Grand in Las Vegas, and Frank was at Caesars Palace. One night before the show, I got a call from Jilly Rizzo, who was Frank's right-hand man. Jilly was a beautiful man, who sadly died very tragically in a car accident a few years after this incident. "Rich, would you like to come over to Caesars Palace after your show? Frank's invited a bunch of entertainers, and he'd like you to be his guest – you know, just sit around, have a few drinks, chew the fat." "Sure, I'd love to," I said.

Brother Chris, Tony Bennett & me: 2000

So, I went on over after my show and sat in the bar waiting for Frank to show up. There were a few other celebrities there, like Vic Damone, Jerry Vale, and a wonderful piano player and close friend, Frankie Randall. When Frank finally arrived, the area was roped off so he could hold court. He did most of the talking. He talked about some of the movies he liked, some of the people he'd worked with – which I loved, of course – and I'd throw out a comment every once in a while. He'd look at me and ask, "How did you know that?" I'd say, "Well, movies are my hobby." At one point, he started to talk about the movie *Guys and Dolls* and what a disappointment it was. He felt it was badly cast. Marlon Brando as Sky Masterson was a joke. Frank told us he'd given Marlon a few singing lessons, to be polite, but it was pretty hopeless. Then he said, "I was miscast in the picture too." Frank played Nathan Detroit, and he said he felt that Sam Levine, who played the role on Broadway, was perfect as Nathan Detroit. "I should have played Sky Masterson." And he should have. Even better, I think Frank should have played Sky Masterson, and Dean Martin should have played Nathan Detroit. But the film was made when Dean wasn't a big enough star yet. And the producer, Sam Goldwyn, probably didn't think Dean on his own was a box office proposition. Anyway, Frank went on and on about what a disappointment the movie was – he didn't think it was well directed, and he didn't think he came off well. While he was talking, we heard a little voice way in the back saying, "You know something, Frank? I liked it. I really did. I liked it. It was a great movie." Frank said, "Who said that?" "It's me," said the voice. "Move back," Frank ordered to those up front, "and let me see who that is." The crowd parted, and there was Tony Bennett, sitting quietly. Frank said, "You liked *Guys and Dolls?*" "It's one of my favorite films, Frank. I watch it all the time. I really like it," Tony said. "Well whaddaya know!" Frank replied. "Why don't you go back to San Francisco and look for your heart? You don't know anything!" Apologetically, Tony said, "I'm sorry, Frank. I just loved the movie. I think it's a classic." Frank wasn't really buying it, and everyone started to laugh. Tony kept saying, "I liked it. I really liked it." About 30 years later, I was in Tony's dressing room when he played at the Paris Hotel in Las Vegas, singing better than ever. I hadn't seen him in years, so I went backstage. He was very gracious, and while we were standing around the bar, I said to Tony, "Do you remember that night many years ago when we got together with Frank over at Caesars and he was talking about his movies?" He replied, "Well, yeah." I continued, "I remember that night because he was talking about *Guys and Dolls*, and you kept saying 'I like it, I like it. It's a great film. It's one of my favorites.' Do you remember saying that, and Frank saying to you, 'Go back to San Francisco and look for your heart?'" He said, "Oh yeah, I remember." "You really like the movie?" I asked. "No, I hate it." "What???" "I hate it. It's a terrible movie. One of the worst movies I've ever seen. It's terrible." "But Tony, you kept saying you liked it, you liked it!" "I know. I was trying to stay in Frank's good graces, trying to butter him up. I wanted to impress him, so I kept saying I liked it. But I hated it. It was an abomination," he concluded.

One of my favorite Frank Sinatra stories took place in Palm Springs when I was doing a benefit for the Barbara Sinatra Children's Center. Gregory Peck was there, and I had a nice chat with him. Bob Hope was also on the bill; and of course, Frank was too, because of Barbara's involvement with the hospital. We were waiting to do sound checks and rehearse with the orchestra, and then we were going to rehearse a number for the end of the show. While we were sitting around, Bob and Barbara were up on stage, looking for Frank to join them. They were supposed to do some dialogue together, and Frank was nowhere to be seen. Barbara asked, "Has anyone seen my husband?" Well, apparently, he'd hidden himself behind some potted plants, and we heard, "Pssst!" We turned around, and there was Frank, behind the bushes, on his hands and knees. He whispered, "Don't tell them where I am. If you do, you're dead meat!" "Why?" we asked. "I don't want to get up there with Bob Hope. I can't stand him. I don't wanna do this, so don't give me away." So, of course, we didn't. Barbara and Bob ended up doing the dialogue without Frank. A little later, we were sitting around talking, and I asked Frank, "What's with you and Bob Hope?" "I can't stand Bob Hope. The guy never paid me or Dean (Martin) for *The Road to Hong Kong*. Remember that movie with Bob and Bing, the last 'Road' picture? Well, Dean and I did a cameo in it. We flew over to England, and he stuck us with the hotel bill. He never paid us. I'm still waiting for the check." I said, "Frank, that was over thirty years ago." "I know. I guess the mail must be slow. Still waiting for my check. The guy's a skinflint." "I thought you and Bob were very close," I offered. "Well, we used to be close, but he's a pain, y'know? I just hope he dies before I do. I'll be able to stand on his grave and dump all his money down onto him. That's what I really want to do." I thought that was a little harsh; but funnily, as it turned out, he did not outlive Bob. I can still remember that image of the great Frank Sinatra hiding from Bob Hope in a bunch of plants, like a little kid, and having us swear we didn't know where he was. He sure was a funny guy.

Over the years, many things have been said about Frank Sinatra, and dozens of books have been written about him. He was a man who genuinely fascinated the public. The more scrapes he got into, the worse he behaved, the more popular he became. The fact that he was thought to be connected with the mob or that he'd get into scuffles with photographers, didn't seem to bother him. It just added to that "bad boy" image, and it made him, in a strange way, much more interesting. But, as I said, I really liked him. I found him interesting, fascinating, and charming. Actually, when he did explode, it was kind of fun to watch; that is, if you weren't the target. He was one of those rare individuals with tremendous charisma. It just goes to prove that if you're a lesser name, not extremely talented, and your behavior's outrageous and unacceptable, you'll disappear from show business. But, if you have the star name and enormous talent, like Frank Sinatra, and the public is fascinated by you and likes you, you can get away with almost anything. And that was Frank.

Hubert Humphrey

A Big Fan

For those of you who aren't old enough to remember, Hubert Humphrey was a senator from Minnesota, who became Lyndon B. Johnson's vice president, and then a Minnesota senator again. He never became president, although he had a good run at it. I joked in my act that Hubert Humphrey never became president because he was under Lyndon Johnson, and Johnson was pretty heavy. Next to Ronald Reagan, Hubert Humphrey had the greatest sense of humor of any politician I have ever met. As with Reagan, you never felt you were in the presence of a man of great prominence. He just seemed to be like the guy next door. I got a lot of mileage out of imitating Hubert Humphrey in the '70s. He was the only vice president I did at that time. He had a very fast-paced, clipped voice, and I loved doing him. Back in the early '70s, Hubert Humphrey and his wife were on *The Merv Griffin Show*. I was also on that show, so I had a great opportunity to do Humphrey in his presence. I got some big laughs and finished to a huge round of applause. Merv asked Muriel Humphrey, "Well, what do you think?" She replied, "I like him better than the old one. I think I'll take him home with me." Needless to say, this got a huge laugh.

Whenever I saw Humphrey socially, he would ask, "Are you still doing me in the act?" I'd say to him, just like I said to Johnny Carson, "Of course." "What are you doing, and what are the jokes?" he'd inquire. I'd answer, "Well, I can't tell you. You'll have to come and see the show." "Does it go over well? Does it get big laughs?" I'd

Vice President Hubert Humphrey & me at the Sands Hotel in Las Vegas

always respond with, "Yeah, you're one of my most popular impressions." In fact, he did come to see me several times when I was performing at the Sands Hotel in Las Vegas. One night, he came backstage just as I was about to go on. He said, "Rich, I'm going to be out there tonight, but I don't want you to change anything. I want to hear it just the way you always do it. Don't cut anything out just because I'm in the audience. I want to hear what you do when I'm not here. I won't be offended – just do what you normally do." I said, "Sure, okay." But to be truthful, I did change a couple of things, a few jokes that were a little strong, but I kept at least 80 percent of the material I did when he wasn't there.

The only time I ever changed an entire routine was years later when Dan Quayle was in the audience. You'll remember he was George Bush, Sr.'s vice president, and he made a number of *faux pas* that the press picked up. In fact, he appeared to be a bit of a dingbat, which he wasn't. The press likes to label people. I capitalized on this, of course, and I had a number of dumb Dan Quayle jokes in the act. When I heard he'd be in the audience, I had to make some major changes. I put all the dumb jokes onto some other politician, but I don't remember exactly who. It wasn't quite as funny, because the other guy didn't have the "dunce" label. When Quayle came backstage, he said, "I loved the act, but I have a sneaking suspicion that you changed a lot of the jokes because I was there." I lied like a snake, "Oh, no, what makes you think that?" I still have the picture we had taken together. On it he wrote, "Dear Rich. Take it easy on me. Dan Quayle." No, he wasn't dumb. He was smart as a whip.

But back to Hubert Humphrey. I had an arrangement with the maître d´ that if Humphrey was in the audience, he was to tell me, and I'd take out a couple of those sensitive jokes. The next time he came, I knew he was there, so I did the "modified" routine. Humphrey came backstage and said, "I'm still not totally convinced. Maybe I'll come and see you one more time. The next time, you won't know I'm out there. I'm going to wear a false beard and a moustache." And we laughed. I said to my manager, "Was he kidding?" We honestly didn't know! I took the precaution of alerting the maître d´: "If you see a man coming in who looks like Hubert Humphrey with a silly moustache and beard, let me know." The very next night, the maître d´ phoned me in my dressing room and said, "I think he's out there. He's wearing a ridiculous looking coat, a pair of glasses and a silly hat. I think it's Hubert Humphrey." I started laughing and sent my road manager, Mel Bishop, out to look. He came back and said, "It's not Hubert Humphrey. It's just some strange-looking guy wearing an old coat, hat, and glasses." I said, "Good thing they didn't kick him out." That reminded me of when I was a kid, and the family saw a strange man at the train station. I said to my dad, "Look at him." And my dad would say, "He's a detective." He did that all the time.

But Hubert Humphrey was really a very likeable man. I was always very fond of him, and it was a shame he never became president; because if he had, I'm sure I would have been at the White House many, many times. Of course, he would never have known. I would have worn a false beard and moustache.

Richard Nixon

I Am Not a Crook!

O f all the voices I've done over the years, none has had more of an impact than that of Richard Nixon. With the possible exception of Ronald Reagan, Nixon's is the voice with which I am most identified. Nixon was a natural. That's because anyone can do Richard Nixon. All you have to do is shake your jowls, make the "V" sign, and say, "I am not a crook!" People have been doing this to me for more than 40 years. Even young people who don't even know who he is do Nixon! If you take a chubby, little baby and shake its jowls with your hand, you have a perfect Nixon! One afternoon, I was driving down Hollywood Boulevard and the fellow in the car next to me recognized me as the guy who imitated Richard Nixon, so he started to shake his jowls and make the "V" sign. He ran into a bus. When I glanced in my rear view mirror, I could see him standing by his damaged car, shaking his jowls and doing the "V" sign for a policeman who was writing it all down.

The first time I met Richard Nixon was in 1973. By this time, I'd done a fair amount of television, and was known primarily as the man who imitated Nixon. I was thrilled to receive an invitation from President and Mrs. Nixon to attend a garden party at the Western White House in San Clemente. Imagine how I felt to be "in" with the elite! On the appointed Sunday afternoon, I drove down to San Clemente with my manager, Gib Kerr. The party was a "thank you" for certain celebrities who had helped him in his re-election campaign. I was amazed at the number of huge stars who were there: Glenn Ford, John Wayne, Glen Campbell, Jimmy Stewart, Jack Benny, George Burns – the list went on and on, all staunch Republicans. My whole act was there! I'd never met my entire act in person, and I shook a number of hands and was delighted that people knew who I was. (Funny, that at most Hollywood parties today, the majority of attendees are Democrats.) Suddenly, Debbie Reynolds, whom I knew only slightly, came over, grabbed my arm, and pulled me around the swimming pool. She was determined to introduce me to Richard Nixon. She dragged me up to

Mr. and Mrs. Nixon, literally threw me at the president, and announced, "Mr. Nixon, Rich Little is going to do you!" Nixon panicked. "Going to do me?" He had no idea what that meant. It was an awkward moment for me, as I stood there a bit bewildered. The next thing I knew, people were gathering around. They'd obviously seen me do Nixon on television and thought, "Oh, this should be fun."

President Richard Nixon & me at his Garden Party in San Clemente – Big smile, but he doesn't know who I am!

Then it suddenly dawned on me. I had to do Richard Nixon, the President of the United States, right there in front of him! If I'd known this was going to happen, I might have prepared a few funny, non-offensive lines, but Debbie had thrown me completely off-guard. Nixon kept looking at me with a "What the heck is going on?" expression, so after a long pause, I started to talk as Richard Nixon. I had no idea where I was going. The lines I used in my act weren't at all appropriate for this situation, so I simply muttered something like, "Mr. President, let me make this perfectly clear. This is a wonderful party you're throwing, and I'm thrilled to be here. Make no mistake about that." Throughout this, I was shaking my jowls and assuming the Nixon persona. Everyone looked at the president, then at me, then back to the president. They weren't about to laugh unless the president laughed. Well, Nixon wasn't laughing. *He had no idea what I was doing.* He just glared at me as I went on and on, and I suddenly realized that *he didn't know I was doing him!* I managed to bring it to an end with something slightly humorous, but no one reacted. There was no applause, but people were gagging themselves trying to hold back the laughter. Nixon was still glaring at me. Then, he turned to his wife, Pat, and said in a loud voice, "Why is this young man speaking in this strange voice?" That got a laugh from the group – they just couldn't help it! He slowly moved away and made no acknowledgement whatsoever that I'd been doing him. I said to myself, "I hope my car is facing north so I can just jump in and head back to Canada. That's it for me. I'm going to be deported." People started talking among themselves, trying to ignore me, and George Burns tried to console me. He said, "Rich, I was so embarrassed, I ate a flower." John Wayne yelled out, "Somebody get a rope!" They were trying to make me feel better, but I wasn't laughing. As Gib and I were trying to make a fast getaway, I was stopped by a Secret Service man, who asked sternly, "Are you Rich Little?" I nodded. He said, "We're going to have to put you under arrest." I thought, "My God! Was my impression of Nixon that bad?" He said, "All Canadians are being deported back to Canada!" Then I realized that the Secret Service men were kidding around with me; they had discovered through Glenn Ford that I was Canadian. They all started laughing, but I wasn't at all amused — for a moment or two I thought it was all too real. We finally made it to the front parking area, our car was brought around, and we hopped in and drove back to Hollywood. Neither of us spoke on the way home. This was my introduction to Richard Nixon. And to this day, whenever I see Debbie Reynolds, I shake my finger at her and call her a little sneak. She giggles. She thought the whole thing was very amusing.

The next time I saw Richard Nixon was at a Mexican restaurant in San Diego, California. Gib and I were eating burritos when we became aware of a commotion in the next room. Apparently, President Nixon had stopped for lunch. I took a peek into the next room, and sure enough, there was President Nixon in a booth with four other guys: one of whom was Bob, the restaurant's owner. I thought for a moment, then decided *not* to go over and say hello. After San Clemente, I thought it would be best to stay as far away from him as possible. Just as I was about to return to my table, I heard the tinkling of glass and the voice I knew only too well. "Excuse me, may I have your attention please!" Nixon continued to tap on the glass until the room became still. Then he stood up. "I hate to interrupt your lunch, but I have an announcement to make." There was dead silence in the room. "Bob, would you please stand up?" Bob stood up looking embarrassed. Nixon said, "Bob, I just want to congratulate you in front of all these people for the excellent beefy taco.

Well done, sir!" Then the rather bewildered customers and servers started to applaud, and Nixon finished with, "Thank you all for your time and cooperation." I guess this was Nixon's way of trying to make some kind of personal contact with his constituents, but he came off as stiff and formal and a bit remote. For years after that incident, if I was in a Mexican restaurant, I'd always ask the waitress to congratulate the cook on an "excellent beefy taco."

I always had a lot of fun imitating Nixon on television, because he was the perfect foil. In one of my sketches, I'd be walking along the beach as Nixon, wearing a blue suit and full Nixon makeup, with Secret Service men walking behind me, erasing my footprints in the sand with palm leaves. Another sketch showed sunbathers in skimpy bathing-suits, slathered with suntan lotion, lying on the beach in Malibu. Cameras panned over to Nixon sitting in a blue suit, shirt and tie, trying to get a suntan. Then, he'd jump up, yawn, and run into the ocean, still wearing his suit.

I found it difficult to do Nixon after Watergate. I didn't like hitting a man when he was down. He was a broken man, and even though he had lied to the nation, there was still a certain amount of sympathy for him. I had to wait at least five years until after he died before I could put him back into my act in a comedic sense. When a celebrity dies, it's okay to do a tribute to him, but it's always wise to wait a decent amount of time before making fun of him again. When someone dies tragically, like John F. Kennedy, it is best never to make fun of them again. Although it's true that time heals all wounds and with changes in comedy today, I suppose Kennedy is fair game.

I guess the problem with Nixon was that he was always a bit of a square. He wasn't warm and friendly like Ronald Reagan. He was more like Ed Sullivan – he laughed when he thought he should and wanted to be one of the guys, but he didn't quite know how to carry it off. Even after all these years, I still do Nixon in my act, although some kids under 30 have no idea what he was like, but they'll laugh because they think he's a funny character. Those of us who lived through the Nixon era, however, will never forget him. He changed this country forever.

George H. W. Bush

A Fun Guy

President George Bush, Sr. & me: 1989

*T*he first time I met George Bush, Sr., I was in Washington, D.C., doing something for Ronald Reagan. My public relations man asked if I would like to meet him. Of course, I did. I was only in town for about three days, and the following day he told me that we had an invitation to go to George Bush's office at two o'clock that afternoon. I said, "Great! Bring your camera." So we were ushered into George Bush's office by his secretary, and he couldn't have been nicer. He knew who I was, had seen me on television many times, and asked if I imitated him. I said, "No, but I'm working on it," which was not true. No one ever does vice-presidents. Nobody knows what they sound like. Don't they just go for coffee? The only vice presidents I ever did were Spiro Agnew, (and I only did him because he had a few scandals going and he was very outspoken, so we heard a lot about him back in the Nixon days). And, I also occasionally did Hubert Humphrey, a person who had a very distinctive speaking style. But those two vice presidents were the exceptions. I did not do George Bush. He then asked me if I had any Gary Hart jokes. Gary Hart was running for president and he'd been caught in a scandal with a young girl. There was a photo in all the newspapers and magazines of this young girl sitting on his knee at a yacht club, and that picture ruined his political career. When something like that happens, something tragic that has sexual overtones, the jokes just fly. Today, they fly on the Internet. Back then, it was from one person to another. I suppose George Bush had heard those jokes from various senators. He started by telling me a couple of slightly blue jokes about Gary Hart; we all laughed, and I thought he had a great sense of humor. But then, why shouldn't he? Growing up in a household full of boys, you'd have to have a great sense of humor.

When George Bush, Sr. was running for president, I was asked by his campaign manager to come to a little fundraiser in Chicago. They wanted a few celebrities there to support Bush, and everyone thought I was a Republican, because I was so friendly with Ronald Reagan. Truth is, I don't really know what I am. I usually vote for the man with the best voice! But then, come to think of it, I didn't vote at all, because at that time, I was a Canadian! In any event, I went to Chicago to support George Bush, Sr. We ended up in a tent somewhere, some kind of cocktail party, with crowds of people milling around. Everyone was chatting and drinking, and I was shaking dozens of hands. People were coming up to me and saying nice things, when suddenly one of Bush's sons (I don't remember who – probably Jeb) said, "Rich, why don't you get up and do a few impressions for us?" I thought, "Oh, my gosh! I'm not really prepared for this, but I do have lines for all the presidents I do in my act. I could do Reagan, then Jimmy Carter, and I'll finish with Nixon." Nixon was still the president I was best known for. The crowd was quite receptive, and things were going well. After I finished doing Richard Nixon, someone in the crowd yelled out, "Do George Bush!" and everyone started to chant, "We want Bush! We want Bush!" I panicked. I did not do George Bush, Sr. I had studied him in person for about 10 minutes,

President George Bush, Sr. & me having a good laugh at the White House

and thought, "This is a tough one. I'll wait to see if he's elected president, and if he is, that's when I'll attempt to work on him." Well, with everyone chanting, "We want Bush! We want Bush!" I thought, "I'm going to have to do something here." And there was

George Bush standing right in front of me. I thought, "Should I say I can't do it and step off the stage? Should I give it a try? Maybe if I have a good joke, they'll laugh at the joke and forget about the impression."

So I had this joke I'd been using in my act for someone else. "I think I'd make a great president. I know the issues: unemployment, inflation, and conservation. Last week I proposed two conservation bills. The first one concerns water, the second one concerns gas. Now if Congress doesn't pass water, then they're sure to pass gas, and I hope they don't make a big stink about it." The joke usually worked no matter who I was impersonating. I just hoped they'd laugh at the joke and not really notice my bad impression of George Bush. Well, there wasn't even a snicker. They didn't even hear the joke. They were just listening for the sound of George Bush. I had laid an egg. I should have quit while I was ahead – with Richard Nixon. As I stepped off the stage, I got some very mild applause. I thought, "This was a dumb move." And I've made plenty of them in my career. To make matters worse, Jeb Bush approached me and said, "Gee, Rich, that really stinks!" I said, "Yeah, it does. I haven't really got him down yet." Jeb said, "No, you haven't.""But listen," I said, "I am going to get your dad down. I promise you. The next time you see me, it'll be close to perfect." He smiled, and we all filed out of the tent. Not much was said for the rest of the visit. But I was true to my word. Six months after George Bush, Sr. was elected president, I had him down pretty good. Dana Carvey was the guy who was known for imitating Bush, but I always thought he sounded more like Mr. Rogers (although he was pretty good). My impression was a little different, and the key was to say things like, "Okay, okay. Gotcha, gotcha. Sure, sure. I understand. No problem," in that jerky little way he had of speaking. It was his nonchalant attitude.

It wasn't long after I had his voice down quite well that I was invited back to Washington, D.C. for another function. George Bush, Sr. was there, and I did him. This time the reaction was much different. Someone took a picture of him shaking my hand, and we were both laughing. I redeemed myself, but I'll never forget that afternoon in Chicago. I was sure glad I never had to get Jeb's voice down!

Ronald Reagan

The Most Loveable President of Them All

Of all the presidents I've known or impersonated, Ronald Reagan was my favorite. He was not only the most interesting president, but a man I got to know and like very much. He was a great listener, and he loved to talk about show business, his career, and other actors and entertainers. I think he got a big kick out of my impersonation of him. Like Richard Nixon, Ronald Reagan was an impersonator's dream. Not only did he have a very distinctive voice, but physically he was ideal. He had a very distinctive walk, he bobbed up and down a lot, and his hands always seemed to hang by his side like meat-hooks. Most people don't remember him as an actor – I certainly didn't. He was never a huge movie star. Most of the movies he'd made since the late '30s were unmemorable, with the possible exceptions of *Knute Rockne All-American* and *Kings Row*. He worked primarily in B movies, and as I was working on my act, I never thought of impersonating him. His voice wasn't that distinctive until he got into politics. He then developed a very specific delivery with slight hesitation, looking down and then looking up, and really connecting with his audience. One time, I asked Reagan why he always looked down before he spoke. He said, "You'd look down too if you owned a horse ranch!"

When he first ran for president, I began to study his voice, and I found him very difficult to impersonate. One day, I ran into a woman at an airport who had been on his staff. She asked if I had mastered the Ronald Reagan impression yet. I said, "Not really, but I'm working on him." She said, "The key to Reagan is 'Well...'" I thought for a moment and realized she was absolutely right! So that was the first hook that I latched onto. A starting point for all impersonations is a hook – a phrase, a gesture, a look – like Clint Eastwood's "Go ahead...make my day" or Arnold Schwarzenegger's "I'll be back!" The hook for Reagan was "Well...." the very same hook I'd used for Jack Benny, and that worked out pretty *well*! It was easy to figure out why Reagan used it so much: it was a stalling tactic. If he was asked a question that he had to think about, he'd look down and say, "Well ..." I think I used it every time "he" opened his mouth!

"Well-Dear Rich – I know one of these fellows is me, but which one? I know I'm not the White Haired One & I hope I'm not wearing the green dress. Warm regards – Ronald Reagan"

The first time I went to the Reagan White House, I was invited, along with several other celebrities, and we were given a tour of the House and grounds. Then Reagan gave a speech at a podium on the White House lawn. It was roped off to the public, but celebrities were allowed to stand in front of the roped-off area. The band played as Reagan stepped up to the podium, with the cameras on him, preparing to make a speech to welcome some foreign dignitary. He scanned the crowd, and his eye caught me standing there next to Fred MacMurray and his wife June Haver. He said, "Well...well...," kidding me, because he'd seen my impersonation of him. "Well...well...," he said again, so I looked back at him and said, as Reagan, "Well...well..." We kept up this exchange for a moment or two until the cameraman signaled to him that he was on national television. He looked up at the camera and said, "I'm so sorry. I didn't know we were on!" And then he said, "Well...," gave a little chuckle, and started his speech. It was quite a thrill for me to know he recognized me.

After his speech, we were introduced formally in the White House, and he told me he'd seen my impersonation of him many times. He asked me what was the key to my impersonation, and I said as Reagan, "Well..." So, off we went again, "Well"ing each other for a good minute or so! Then he asked me which movie stars I liked to impersonate. When I told him Jimmy Stewart, he immediately went into his own Jimmy Stewart impression. It wasn't too bad – I'd heard worse. Then he did John Wayne – also not too bad. But his Truman Capote really threw me for a loop. Who would expect to hear the President of the United States doing a Truman Capote impersonation! He rubbed his eyes, put his head back, and started to talk in that raspy little Truman Capote voice. Then he asked, "What do you think?" I said, "That was pretty good." "Thanks, but I really don't have a joke. I need something to say as Truman Capote," he replied. "Well, I'll give you a joke I use in my act," I said. "Great," said Reagan. "Let me get this down." He took a piece of paper and prepared to write the joke down on the back of the Secret Service man standing next to him. I said, "Hi, fun seekers, this is Truman Capote. You know, a lot of people think I wrote *In Cold Blood*. Well, that's not true. Actually, I wrote in ink." Reagan beamed. He loved the joke. "Can I use that?" "Sure," I said, "It's yours."

"Thanks, Rich. You're a pal," he chuckled. "I can't wait to try that on Gorbachev." Every time I think of that, I start to laugh. I can't imagine telling that to Gorbachev!

On one visit to the White House, I was seated between Nancy and the president in the East Room (I wasn't performing that night). When the entertainment concluded, everyone stood up to leave, but protocol demanded that no one leave the room before the president, so they all had to stand waiting for his lead. He suddenly started to talk to me about *Desperate Journey,* a movie he'd made with Errol Flynn, Alan Hale, Sr., and Arthur Kennedy back in the '40s. It was directed by Raoul Walsh, one of the great directors of the time. "So the four of us were down in this little gully, and when the director called, 'Action!' we were supposed to come up over a hill. While we were waiting for our cue and they were setting up the lights and so on, we noticed that Errol was kicking up the dirt in front of him. I finally figured out what he was doing. When the director called, 'Action!' and we moved out of the gully and up over the hill, he would appear taller than we were! Well, we would have none of that, so we started kicking up dirt too! Then when Walsh finally called, 'Action!' and we came up over the hill, we were so tall, that the camera cut our heads off! Walsh was furious! He saw the dirt, and started yelling, 'What are you guys doing? We're trying to make a movie here! Stop fooling around! We'll break for lunch now and do this shot again when we get back.' After lunch when we were getting ready to do the scene again, we noticed Flynn had a ladies' bonnet in his hand. Well, we weren't going to be upstaged by that, so we went to wardrobe and got bonnets too. This time when Walsh called, 'Action!' we all came up over the hill wearing bonnets! Walsh went crazy! He screamed, 'Are you guys *trying* to ruin this picture? You're costing me money! I think this is your doing, Flynn. Another display like this, and you're off the picture!' Flynn replied, 'Is that a promise, old boy?' We got back into the gully. This time, when Walsh said, 'Action!' Alan Hale, Arthur Kennedy and I came up over the hill in our uniforms. Errol Flynn came up totally naked!" Reagan thought this was quite amusing (it was!), but it took him six or seven minutes to tell this whole story with all the details, while his guests were all standing there waiting for him to leave the room. Finally, as he started into yet another story, Nancy tapped him on the shoulder and said, "Dear, we really must go. The people …" He looked around and said, "Oh, I'm so sorry!" When we finally left the East Room, he was still talking about Errol Flynn and all the escapades he got into during his film career.

Reagan loved to talk about movies. One time, Nancy asked me what my favorite movie was. I said, "*The Best Years of Our Lives.*" She said that was one of her favorites too. "What's your favorite Ronald Reagan picture," she asked. I replied, "*Kings Row.* What's your favorite?" She

President, Nancy Reagan & me moments before the seal I stuck on the podium fell off!

thought for a moment, took Reagan's arm, and said, "Our wedding picture!"

Another time at the White House, I was seated next to the president as we watched a magician by the name of Harry Blackstone, Jr. go through his routine. He was an excellent magician – did a lot of sleight of hand

and some very good card tricks. I told the president that I knew a fair amount of magic just from standing backstage and watching various acts when I was performing in variety shows, but I wasn't an expert by any means. He asked, "What's the secret? What's the key to doing magic?" I really didn't have an answer for him, because every illusion is different. We continued watching Harry set up for some fairly big illusion in which he made someone disappear. Reagan was enthralled by the whole thing. "How does he do that?" I concluded, "Well, Mr. President, I'd say the person who disappears, usually an assistant or someone very small, gets into the base of the apparatus and just squinches down or rolls his or herself up so it looks like it's empty. It's not true in every case, but usually they're in the base." He nodded, "Ah, so that's how it's done." Nancy arrived to join us as we watched Harry do some "pick a card" tricks. He had the president pick a card and put it back into the deck. Harry then picked up a lemon, which he cut open to reveal the very card the president had picked. As everyone applauded, Nancy turned to Reagan and asked, "How did he do that?" And Reagan replied, "It's simple. It's in the base!"

I'd always bring my own props to the White House. I'd bring a podium too, because Reagan behind a podium was kind of a signature look. I even had my own presidential seal on the podium, which read, "In Rich We Trust." Reagan once said to me, "That's a great looking seal." I said, "We should have one of those made with 'In Ron We Trust.'" He'd often stand up after I'd done my act and turn to the audience with, "Well…," and then he'd proceed to do some of the material I had already done. The audience just loved it. He had a wonderful sense of humor, and I was never concerned about performing in front of him, even though some of his aides worried about what I might say. They'd hover around before I went on, worried that I might say something too racy or make some criticism of his administration, but I never cleared any material with them. If, on occasion, I'd say something with a slight sexual connotation, they'd all look like they had just swallowed a basketball. They'd look over at the president, who'd be screaming with laughter. Then, of course, they'd start laughing too.

Reagan could take great kidding about himself. I never had to

President Ronald Reagan & me – He loved to laugh at a good joke.

worry about Reagan jokes, even if they were about his memory or his age, because he'd just throw back his head and roar with laughter. He was my best audience!

One afternoon, I got caught in traffic on my way to tea at the White House, and I was really worried about arriving late. As I finally walked down the corridor, I saw the president talking to the press. They were firing questions at him, and I could see he wasn't too happy about this. He wanted to get to his private quarters and have tea and sandwiches with his friends, but the Grenada crisis had just broken out, and he had to deal with a barrage of very strong questions. He was doing his best, but when he saw me approach, he called out, "Rich, thank God you're here. You do me better than I do. You finish this damned press conference. I'm going for a sandwich." And, with that, he split. Just before he disappeared into the Oval Office, he turned around and yelled, "And for God's sake, Rich, don't get us into a war!" Would you believe the press just gathered around me and started to ask the same questions! I couldn't take anything seriously – after all, what did I know about foreign policy? So when they asked me about Grenada, I just said, "I think it's the finest tune Buddy Greco has ever recorded." I kept answering in this vein and the press guys were writing everything down. They kept asking questions like they were still talking to Reagan. A few minutes later, Reagan, with a cup of tea and a sandwich in his hand, stuck his head out and said, "You're doing great. Keep it going!" The next question from the press was, "Do you think the government's ever going to legalize marijuana?" I said, "No, but we're going to discuss it next week during a joint session!" I got another "thumbs up" sign from Reagan. Then someone asked, "With all the unrest in the Middle East, do you think you'll send jets to Israel?" I replied, "No, what would they do with a bunch of football players?" Reagan loved this whole bit. He got a huge kick out of the whole thing. Much later, he said, "I should have you with me all the time, then I wouldn't have to talk so much. You could do it for me."

I think my funniest Reagan moment occurred when my then-wife, Jeanne, and I were invited to the White House for a reception in honor of the President of Sri Lanka. It took place in the East Room, and there were several speakers before the Pres-

The President of Sri Lanka, his wife & President Reagan at the White House watching me do my impression of Oliver Hardy

ident of Sri Lanka rose to make his speech. This man was straight out of Central Casting. He looked like a cross between Peter Sellers and Peter Ustinov. I settled in for a long, boring speech, but to my surprise he started talking about Laurel and Hardy! I looked over at President Reagan, and he was beaming. This certainly had grabbed his interest. He leaned over to me and said, "My kind of guy!" The President of Sri Lanka told us that most of what he knew about the United States came from watching Laurel and Hardy films. They were very popular in his country and most Sri Lankans looked on them as quintessential Americans. The president was in his element – at least he didn't have to listen to some boring political diatribe. He applauded the speech with great vigor, beaming with pleasure. After the speech, Jeanne and I joined the president and his guest from Sri Lanka at the reception. Reagan told the president, "What a coincidence that you like Laurel and Hardy. I was one of their biggest fans. I saw every picture they ever made, and I'm a bit of an authority on Laurel and Hardy." The President of Sri Lanka nodded his head, and Jeanne and I waited for Reagan to continue. "My favorite of all their routines is 'Who's on first?' I think it's one of the funniest routines I've ever seen." Well, there was a brief silence as Jeanne looked over at me as if to say, "Don't say a word. Please don't say a word." We both realized that Reagan had the wrong comics. "Who's on first?" was Bud Abbott and Lou Costello's most famous routine. The president repeated himself, "Yes, 'Who's on first?' is my absolute favorite of all the Laurel and Hardy routines." The President of Sri Lanka said, "What?" And President Reagan came back with, "No, he was on second. Who was on first." The President of Sri Lanka said, "I'm sorry, I don't understand." For a brief moment, I thought Reagan was going to say, "Understand? No he was the shortstop." But, thankfully, he didn't. Just listening to the two presidents doing this "Who's on first?" routine at complete cross-purposes was one of my better moments at the White House.

About this next account, the people who were there will vouch for the fact that the following story is true, even though some will find it hard to believe.

One of the greatest thrills of my life was to be invited to perform at President Reagan's first Inaugural Gala. Some of the greatest names in show business were there. I knew Patricia Neal, the great actress best known for her Academy Award-winning performance in *Hud,* and who also made a picture with Reagan called *The Hasty Heart* – a delightful lady. Tom Selleck and Elizabeth Taylor were there too. After the swearing-in was over, we had a little break before going to the first presidential ball, so we went over to Patricia Neal's suite at the Watergate Hotel. We relaxed and had a drink, killing time before the reception. Patricia Neal suddenly said, "Rich, why don't you call Bette Davis? She should have been here. Call her as Jimmy Stewart and ask her why she isn't here." I said, "Sounds like a good gag, but I don't know Bette Davis. I'd be too uptight. She frightens me." Pat said, "No, no – she's great. She'll get a kick out of it. You could fool her with Jimmy." "No, I'd be too terrified. I don't think so," I insisted. But, she was already dialing the number and Bette answered immediately. She handed me the phone, and I had no choice but to launch into my Jimmy Stewart impersonation. She bought it, totally, right off the top. I told her how we missed her at the inauguration, and that President Reagan had asked after her. She kept saying, "How nice of you to call. You're such a sweet man, and we had such fun making that movie together, *Right of Way* for HBO." I kept rambling on as Jimmy Stewart, and thought, "How am I going to get out of this? Bette was so convinced, she started to get personal, and said, "Don't forget, you're coming up to the house in July. Are you bringing the kids?" Of course, I had no idea what she was talking about, and I knew I was in way over my head, so I finally said, "Miss Davis, we're just putting you on. My name is Rich Little and I'm not really Jimmy Stewart." There was a very long pause. I said, "Miss Davis, I hope you're not upset." She yelled, "This is outrageous! How dare you do this to me?" I said, "Miss Davis, it's just a joke." She said, "Well, I don't find it funny. I don't find it at all funny! I am furious!" At which point she slammed down the receiver. I felt terrible. I thought, "I hope I never run into this lady, because my name's gotta be mud with her now."

What started out as an amusing little prank turned into something

Me & President Ronald Reagan

that left us all feeling kind of down. No one said much as we made our way to the ball. The first person we saw when we walked into the reception was Jimmy Stewart, talking to the president. Pat walked right up to them and told them what had happened. They were quite enthralled by the whole thing, particularly Jimmy. "Really? You did me? That's great, because you do me so well. Bette must have gotten a real kick out of it." I said, "No, she most definitely did not get a kick out of it." The president asked, "She didn't find it funny?" I replied, "Nooo! She was mad. She swore at me and she hung up." President Reagan said, "Why, that doesn't sound like her at all. I know she's a tough old bird, but she's always had a good sense of humor. I find this so hard to believe." I added, "Well, it's all my fault." And the president said, "Don't be so hard on yourself. It probably isn't as bad as you think." I said, "Mr. President, she was really not pleased." Jimmy said, "We'll just have to straighten it out." Reagan agreed, but I said, "Don't worry about it, Mr. President. This is your Inauguration Day. You don't have time for this. It's forgotten." Reagan said, "No, it isn't. Come with me. We'll find a phone and straighten this out. Maybe she isn't feeling well." I was pretty impressed that the president would take time out of his important day to try to mend this fence, but he was quite adamant about it. We found a phone in a quiet area, Pat gave him the number, and President Reagan asked the switchboard to be put through. Bette came on the phone immediately. "Hello, Bette. This is Ron." Bette Davis said, "Fuck you, Rich Little!" and hung up on the President of the United States. The President put the phone back very softly. And everyone asked, "What did she say?" "She told me to fuck off!"

As we were leaving, Jimmy said, "I'll phone her next week and straighten it all out." "Jim, do me a favor," I said, "don't ever bring this up again, because she swore at me, and she swore at the president. Let's just leave it at that. It'll only get worse." I don't know if Jimmy ever told her the truth – I doubt it, because he was a true gentleman, and he would not have wanted to embarrass her. But I do often wonder if Bette Davis realized that she told the President of the United States to fuck off!

I liked Ronald Reagan. He was like the loveable, old grandfather you perhaps never had, the next door neighbor you could tell a joke to, the pal you could confide in. He was always good-natured – so much so that when I was with him, I never really felt I was with the President of the United States. I know many people felt that way. Certainly, of all the presidents I've met, Ronald Reagan was the most personable.

Rich with President Bill Clinton

Rich portraying Presidents Reagan, Johnson & Nixon for the play "The Presidents" 2002

Rich with President George W. Bush at the White House

Hal Linden,
Ricardo Montalbán
& Rich

Muhammad Ali & Rich

Mikhail Baryshnikov,
Don Rickles & Rich

Charleton Heston & Rich

Rich meeting (R-L): Princess Diana, Prince Charles & Prime Minister Brian Mulroney

Rich & Robert Stack

*Angie Dickenson
& Rich*

*Rich with
Bryan Cranston*

*Rich &
Carol Burnett
at the
"Indy 500"*

*Rich &
Tony Orlando:
2015*

Ruta Lee & Rich

*Rich as Jimmy Stewart in his
play "Jimmy Stewart & Friends"
2014*

Rich & Suzanne Somers:
2015

Rich under his street sign
in Ottawa, Canada

Gerald McRaney, Rich &
Gary Sinise
Washington, D.C.:2014

Rich with Ann Miller, June Allyson & Vikki Car at the Sands Hotel

Rich receives star with Marie Little for the Las Vegas Walk of Stars: 2005

Rich Little
"Maestro of Impression"

Rich & Clint Eastwood

*The Little Family: (L-R)
Robin, Fred, Elizabeth,
Dorothy McKay (aunt),
Chris and Rich*

*Rich and Catherine Little at Rich's
star (received 1998) at the Palm
Springs Walk of Stars*

*Rich with friends: (L-R) Arlene & Dick Van
Dyke, Ray & Karen Stone, and Laura & Ed
Gillespie*

*Rich & Jeanne
on one of their
first dates
(We haven't
changed,
have we?
Well, maybe
the clothes!)*

*Catherine with Rich
(not pictured) in
San Francisco
(No one noticed me.
I wonder why?)*

Rich with friends: (L-R) Bob Betley, Steve Rossi & Jane Betley

Rich as Ross Perot (for a commercial)

Rich with his one-eyed cat T-Bo

Memories

I've been very blessed in my career to meet so many interesting and talented people. Some people come in and out of your life, and you don't even really remember they were there. They don't make any real impression on you. Others you may only meet once, but you will always remember them because you admired them so much. You remember every detail of your meeting, just as I remember Alan Ladd signing that picture I drew of him early one Monday morning in Ottawa so many years ago. Because he was such an idol of mine, I remember every single moment of that experience. I'm sure he didn't.

The people who have impressed me the most are those who are not only talented, but who treat people the way you yourself treat others – or at least try to. That's why I remember:

- Ricardo Montalbán. I did a number of *Fantasy Island* episodes back in the '70s. He gave me many tips to be a better actor.

- Lou Gossett, Jr., whom I knew for a short time when I lived in Malibu. He was very down to Earth.

- Hal Linden – one of the best.

- Claire Trevor, a big star in the '30s and '40s, who lived in Newport, California. She was a terrific lady, a great actress, a talented painter, and would only get together with me if I imitated John Wayne, Humphrey Bogart or Edward G. Robinson. They were her all-time favorites. She had worked with them all.

- Rosemary Clooney, a wonderful singer and a real sweetheart; and her brother Nick, George Clooney's father, who is a good friend of mine. George got his sense of humor from him.

- Barry Morse, who I knew from Canada, played Inspector Gerard on *The Fugitive*.

- E. W. Swackhamer, who was the director of *Love on a Rooftop*, a series in which I appeared as the wacky next door neighbor. I told him I played a caterpillar in a children's play when I was 9.

- Herb Voland, who played the father on that series. What a role model!

- George Kirby, who was very, very helpful to me in my early days in show business, teaching me how to do impressions – if you can do such a thing!

- Greg Garrison, who produced and directed *The Dean Martin Show* and *The Dean Martin Celebrity Roasts*. He always phoned me after each show to tell me what he had to cut from my routine!

- Paul Keyes, who produced and directed the *Variety Club* television tributes in the '70's.

- Jon Voight, a great actor, a staunch Republican, and great supporter of our troops and firemen.

- Phil Harris, who wouldn't talk to me unless I did Jack Benny for him.

- George W. Bush, as president, he was a man with many problems. But as a person, he was fun, charming, and personable, with a great sense of humor.

- Shirley MacLaine, a bright and interesting lady. Sometimes a little off the wall, but that's what I like about her.

- Clint Eastwood, a very humble and talented man. Can you think of any director at his age that is as good? Remarkable.

Epilogue

I've Done More Than a 'Little' With My Life...

*F*ew people can look back on their lives with the satisfaction of knowing that their dreams have come true. I was born and brought up in a mid-sized city in Canada, and I became one of the best-known impressionists in the world. It didn't come easily, but I recognized the talents that God gave me, and I knew I had to do them justice. The little boy from Canada made it to the big time.

Me & my mum

On the very first flight I took from Canada to the United States, the stewardess asked if I wanted a shrimp cocktail. I declined. I told her I didn't drink. She explained that she was offering me an appetizer of shrimp with cocktail sauce. We never had this kind of food in our house; my mum always made celery soup. So, I tried the shrimp cocktail, and boy, did I love it! From that time on, I would save up to buy shrimp, and my dad would chide me for wasting my money. Until the day he died, he could never understand why I would spend $2.50 for shrimp when my mum could make a whole pot of celery soup for the same amount of money and feed a family of five. When I was a kid, all we ever had for lunch was celery soup. Today, I never eat celery soup.

My mother was 94 when she passed away. She had a full life and was more than proud of her three sons. My father passed away before I became well known, so he never saw my success. I wish he could have seen how my life turned out, because it was his influence that guided me throughout my career. He gave me the foundation for who I am today. In my eyes, he's my biggest star.

There were three boys in the Little family: Fred was the oldest, I was in the middle, and then there was Chris.

Fred, me, mum & Chris

Chris Little painting

Fred started out as a social worker and then later went into show business. He did animated cartoon voices; I think they were even better than the originals. He was amazing. Had he had the right connections and a few breaks, he could have been very successful. It also helps to be in the right place at the right time.

My younger brother, Chris, was a brilliant artist. Unfortunately, he passed away when he was only in his fifties. I believe that if he had lived, he would have become a world-class painter.

These days, I live in Las Vegas, Nevada, with my little one-eyed tabby, T-Bo. My heart, though, will always be with Dudley — a beautiful sheepdog who was my sidekick on my television show in the '70s. He received more fan mail than I did! I guess that's why the show was cancelled! They never did a show with him.

When I look back on my life, I think show business was easy — relationships were hard. I'm not proud to say that I've been married four

Me, Bria & Jeanne – Christmas card

Daughter Bria & me

Me & daughter Lyndsay

times. At most of my weddings, they threw Minute Rice.

My first wife, Jeanne Worden, is a wonderful lady. I was married to her for 18 years. We first met when I was slated to be a guest on *The Joey Bishop Show.* Jeanne was Joey Bishop's secretary at the time. She came down to the studio during rehearsal to meet another guest: Engelbert Humperdinck. She was a fan. I guess I have him to thank that we ended up together, because that's how I got to meet her. Jeanne had a great sense of business. We were a fabulous team. After an engagement at a hotel, she took my check and opened up my first bank account for me, as well as finding me a great business agent, Perry Potkin. In those days, I ended up working a great deal and being gone most of the time. Although it was terrific for my career, it was not so good for my marriage. Consequently, I was not a great husband. However, our daughter, Bria, turned out just fine. She lives in Malibu, California, with her dog Elsie and her boyfriend James, a talented, young singer. She is smart, bright, fun, adventurous, loving, and passionate.

She inherited her mother's good looks, and she definitely got my sense of humor. I adore her and am happy that her mother and I are friends.

I also have a second daughter, Lyndsay, who is a love child. She currently resides in Las Vegas, Nevada, with her mother, after relocating from Delaware. She's a shy, caring person, and a wonderful mother to my adorable granddaughter, Alaina, who is six.

My second wife, Jeannette Markey, was also an entertainer. The marriage was short-lived. She was more interested in pursuing her career than being a wife.

I would have only been married three times, but my third wife passed away in 2010 after a long illness. Marie (Marotta) was the love of my life. She was bright, beautiful, had a great sense of humor, was a former dancer, and became a great wife and business partner. Marie did everything for me: she took care of me, wrote for me, travelled with me, and advised me with my investments. She made a lot of money for me, and was always by my side. I miss her every day.

Granddaughter Alaina

Jeannette, Frank Sinatra & me

Me & Marie – the love of my life

Catherine & me

I was briefly married to Catherine Brown, who remains a good and loyal friend and is very close to my daughter Lyndsay. That marriage should have worked. She was by my best friend, Steve Rossi's bedside every day after he was diagnosed with cancer, until he died. Bless her. I still see a lot of Catherine and her two wonderful boys, Shane and Ty.

As for the business side, when it comes to money, you have to be very careful. I believe that many entertainers who have been successful in the entertainment industry have had people steal from them. You must be extremely cautious about who has access to your financial information and who handles your money. Over the years, I've had dishonest people I thought I could trust steal millions from me. I am fortunate to have two people in my life now who I not only trust, but who do an outstanding job taking care of me: Jeri Fischer, my business manager, financial and investment advisor – the rock in my life; and Dāna Stern, who administrates my company, handles the entertainment business, and is my go-to for "technical difficulties." Both of them look after me personally. They are not only excellent employees, but good friends as well.

I've told you a little about my personal life, but this is not really a biography. I didn't marry anyone famous, and I've led a relatively quiet life – except for the fact that I've met and worked with some of the greatest names in show business and several United States Presidents. Most are not with us anymore. In fact, many young people today might not even know who they are: Judy Garland, Bing Crosby, Jackie Gleason, Lucille Ball, Jack Benny, Richard Nixon, and Frank Sinatra to name a few. While it's true that I've liked and admired most of them (as evidenced by many of their stories here), this is not to say there weren't a few that I wasn't crazy about. There were those who were stereotypically arrogant, cold, and self-absorbed – but I don't want to talk about Wayne Newton, Joey Bishop, Buddy Greco, and Roseanne Barr. Fortunately, they were in the minority. The stars I was really close with were Jimmy Stewart, Ronald Reagan, Mel Tormé, Stewart Granger, Robert Goulet, Howard Keel, and Steve Rossi.

Steve Rossi & me

Steve Rossi was half of that great former comedy team Allen and Rossi. They were very popular back in the '60s. Steve was my dearest and closest friend – funny, loyal, giving – and thought the way I do. He turned almost everything into comedic form. In fact, since we were together so much, people thought we were the new comedy team. But that would never have happened, because Steve would've wanted top billing! Steve is not with us anymore, but he will always have a very special and warm place in my heart.

Herb Stott & me

My other really close friends are Herb Stott and Gord Atkinson. Herb lives in Hollywood, California. I've known Herb for more than 40 years. He was a commercial director, and we met when he directed me in about 20 commercials for television: Little Debbie snack cakes, Thrifty Car Rental, Pizza Hut, Ace Hardware, and many more. Herb has a wonderful, sarcastic sense of humor and has always been there for me.

But Gord Atkinson is the man I've known the longest – 60 years. Gord was my boss when I was a disc jockey back in my hometown of Ottawa, Canada. I worked at radio station CFRA back in the '50s. I think

Me & Gord Atkinson

they actually hired me because I could save the station a lot of money. They knew I did a variety of voices. I did my own show as me, read the news as David Brinkley, the commentaries as Walter Cronkite, the teen show as Elvis, and the sports as Howard Cosell. However, I only got one salary. So, I quit! When I was a teenager, Gord was responsible for jump-starting both my and Paul Anka's careers (though Paul seems to have forgotten that). Gord played my records on his show, interviewed me, and encouraged me to move to the United States to become a full-time impersonator, the same thing he did for Paul. He is a man of immense loyalty and integrity. He is a much-trusted and treasured friend.

Jeri Fischer, me, Dāna Stern, Chuck Hoover & Laurie Caceres

I also want to acknowledge a few people who have been instrumental in my career, and who have also become good friends: Mel Bishop, my former road manager who was like a brother; Chuck Hoover, my musical director and pianist; Laurie Caceres, my show production and video manager; and Mike Pick, my booking agent – people I can always rely on.

They say if you have three close friends, you are doing well. Well, I have hundreds of friends because I talk to myself all the time! I sing in the shower as Sinatra, drive my car like Kirk Douglas, and make love as Truman Capote. Yet, I have two children. Interesting? And back then, one of my best impressions was Johnny Carson. No wonder I was married four times!

These days, I still perform and love it as much as ever. I don't work as much as I used to, but in the past several years, I've written and starred in a one-man play based on the life of Jimmy Stewart called *Jimmy Stewart & Friends.* Besides sincerely admiring the man in both his career and personal life, I considered Jimmy a dear friend and am currently on the Board of Directors for his museum in Indiana, Pennsylvania. I performed this play touring around the country and Canada for several years before settling in at the LVH Hotel (formerly the Hilton, currently the Westgate) in Las Vegas, where the show resided for over a year.

I'm currently performing *Rich Little Live!*, an abbreviated version of my new show, *Little by Little* (my own life's story with many impressions, complete with behind-the-scene stories and videos), at the Laugh Factory in the New Tropicana Hotel & Casino in Las Vegas, since July 2015, as well as performing it around the country. I'm also working on my show as a play adaptation. If all goes well, I plan on taking *Little by Little* to Broadway. This is one of my life-long dreams.

Me with President Jimmy Carter singing "Happy Birthday" to him

There are also a few memorable occasions whose significance stands out for me. In 2005, I was honored to be invited to entertain at the Inaugural Ball for President George W. Bush. In 2006, I was invited to perform on the *Late Show with David Letterman*, and was thrilled to learn that that particular show earned the highest ratings of the season. In April 2007, I performed at the White House Correspondents Dinner. The press loved it. That is, the ones that were listening. And several years ago, I had fun singing happy birthday to Jimmy Carter – in his voice. When I finished, I said to him, "Now, wasn't that sweeter than Marilyn Monroe?"

From the fall of 2007 to early 2008, I returned to headline at the Golden Nugget Hotel in Las Vegas after almost 20 years. It was a blast. I would have stayed longer, but I had to leave because of an illness – everyone was sick of me. (Just kidding!) I became very ill. What I thought was pneumonia, turned out to be a blood clot, and I had to stop performing for a while.

Me & Marie after helping the homeless

I've been very blessed throughout my life, and have strongly believed in giving back. And, as a result, I have always supported many worthwhile causes and organizations. My late wife, Marie, was extremely passionate about helping others and paying it forward, especially when it came to children, animals and the homeless. We set up a philanthropic trust which sponsors many worthwhile organizations. The Marie and Rich Little Foundation donated funds to establish the Marie Little Spay and Neuter Clinic at the Heaven Can Wait Animal Sanctuary. Our annual benefit supports not only Heaven Can Wait, but the Salvation Army of Southern Nevada, the Las Vegas Rescue Mission, and all their wonderful programs. There is the Rich Little Special Care Nursery in Ottawa, Canada; I was presented with the Key to the City for this effort. I donate 100% percent of all the proceeds from my shows' merchandise sales to the Gary Sinise Foundation for our troops, and do special charitable performances throughout the year for all branches of the Armed Forces, as well as participating in numerous fundraisers each year to help other charitable causes.

There are many people to whom I'm indebted for my success. Some are portrayed in this book. After many decades of performing as an impersonator, I can truly say I have lived a full and exciting life. I'm grateful to my family and friends and all those who helped me for their love and support down through the years.

AFTERWORD

or more than five decades, Ottawa-born Rich Little has entertained millions of fans with his impressions of past and present celebrities. While he is best known for his stand-up impressions of famous people, his latest creative venture will see him starring in a one-man show destined for Broadway, featuring his own life and career.

His ability to come close to "becoming" the celebrity he is presenting has amazed his fans and friends since the beginning of his career. Watching him perform, audience members often forget that it's Rich Little, and almost believe they are watching George Burns, Jack Nicholson or Willie Nelson! His uncanny ability to recreate not only the voices and inflections of the characters, but also their unique body language, creates a complete impression, right before your eyes!

Rich played all the roles in a television special, *Rich Little's Christmas Carol*, based on the Charles Dickens classic. Awarded the Montreux Festival Award in Switzerland, as well as an international Emmy, this classic has been released on DVD with an additional bonus feature, *Rich Little's Robin Hood*, and a conversation with director Trevor Evans.

Over the many successful years of his career, Rich has appeared regularly with Ed Sullivan, Jackie Gleason, Glen Campbell and Dean Martin, and has appeared on *Laugh-In, The Julie Andrews Show* and, at one time, starred in his own television variety show. He was named comedy star of the year by the American Guild of Variety Artists, and his impressions of Johnny Carson were so memorable that he portrayed Johnny in an HBO movie entitled *The Late Shift*.

He has appeared in a couple of major Hollywood movies, and his career continues to flourish. He headlined at several hotels and casinos in Las Vegas, Nevada, where he entertained his full-house audiences with the voices of famous super-stars and presidents. He's now showcasing his newest project, "Rich Little Live!" also in Las Vegas, adding yet the latest crop of celebrities to his incredible repertoire, along with rare, vintage video clips.

But his real love is donating his time and talent to the many charitable causes he supports. Rich was co-host of the Canadian Division of the Children's Miracle Network, the Las Vegas Heart Association, Northern California Burn Association, Through the Eyes of a Child Foundation, Ronald McDonald House, Keepers of the Wild, the National Kidney Foundation, and more than a dozen other worthy causes and organizations. He has also been inducted into the Miami Children's Hospital International Pediatrics Hall of Fame.

Part of his sense of duty and sharing includes his USO tours in support of the troops on duty in far-off postings, along with his musical director Chuck Hoover, his band members and the amazing Kathy Walker, a fellow impersonator.

A conversation with Rich Little is a little like being at a cocktail party with the most influential, entertaining and interesting people of the 20th and 21st centuries. Recently, I caught up with Rich and we sat down to catch up on his life, passions and latest ventures.

Ray: "You're well known around the world for your incredible impressions of famous people, but, back home in Ottawa, folks know the other side of Rich Little. For instance, you were instrumental in opening the Rich Little Special Care Nursery at the Ottawa Hospital, along with Frank Sinatra and many private donors from the Ottawa area."

Rich: "I was born in the Civic Hospital (now the civic campus of the Ottawa Hospital) and they're still looking for the stork that delivered me. My father was a doctor in Ottawa, so that hospital and the Special Care Nursery have always had a special place in my heart. In fact, I visit the nursery every chance I get when I'm there. I also came to Ottawa back in the '70s to appear in a television special to raise funds for the United Way with Larry Mann, Lloyd Bochner and several Canadian headliners."

Ray: "Where did it all start?"

Rich: "Well, when I was a kid and discovered that I could imitate the voices of some of my teachers. It got a lot of laughs, and that's when the audience bug bit me. I later found out that if I phoned any girl I was interested in and imitated the voice of her favorite actor, it made a great impression — if you'll excuse the expression. A few years later, when I was 18 years old, I got into radio using those talents. Who knew I'd get paid for that?"

Ray: "You had quite a run with the Ottawa Little Theatre back then."

Rich: "I had a swell time performing on that stage. It was quite an experience performing with so many talented actors in over 40 productions. I learned a lot about the profession. It was about that time that I recorded my first comedy album *My Fellow Canadians*. Obviously, that album featured many of the hot politicians of that era, and actually became a bestseller."

Ray: "Actually, it became the best selling comedy album in Canadian history!"

Rich: "One of my most wonderful memories was an evening at the National Arts Centre. It was my birthday and Mel Tormé showed up on stage with a big birthday cake. Mel did a great show, and it was such an honor to be working with him. Mel was a great movie buff, and such a good friend. We had a great rapport, and it was terrific to have him on the show." *(Breaks into Mel Tormé voice: "Chestnuts Roasting on an Open Fire")* "I had an interesting experience involving David Niven. I did his voice for two of his last films: *The Trail of the Pink Panther* and *The Return of the Pink Panther*. What a great honor to do those films. Blake Edwards, Julie Andrews' husband, directed and produced those films, and he called me on the phone and asked, 'Do you do David Niven?' I said, 'No, not really. Why?' Blake said, 'He's losing his voice and we've had him in the studio trying to fix it by re-recording him, and it's worse than it was when we shot it. His voice is gone. I can't make out anything he says! We've shot this movie with Capucine and Robert Wagner and we just let David say his lines but we can't understand anything he's saying.' I felt really bad for him, so I went to the studio to record his lines, and the hard part was when I was trying to put my voice into his lips. It took hours to do it. *(Switches to David Niven voice)* After I did my David Niven role, I asked Blake Edwards to go and tell David I'd be very happy to go to Spain and follow him around for day-to-day conversation, so he could talk to people. I'd be very honored to do that. I got a lovely card from him saying, '*Rich, you saved my life. You made the picture work for me, and I'll always be indebted to you.*' But I never met him! I also dubbed for Peter Sellers in the same movie, because he was gone by then too."

Ray: "You were a frequent guest on *The Tonight Show* with Johnny Carson, and eventually became a regular replacement host for him when he was away."

Rich: "Yes. I replaced Johnny Carson many times as host; and I used to get so deeply into the Carson impressions, that when I finished doing the show, I would find myself going to the dressing room and writing out an alimony check. I do Carson and Carnac in my own shows; and, after all these years, whenever I do Johnny, it still gets a great reaction. In my opinion, he was the best television host that ever lived, and a great guy. I still admire his mannerisms and the way he could make every situation funny."

Ray: "You got a lot of publicity when you were the star of the U.S. President's 2007 Washington Press Club annual dinner."

Rich: "That was a special honor, and the show was anticlimactic, because it was a tough audience. Oh, my gosh, they were tough. I threw out a lot of material I had prepared. A lot of people didn't listen. It was a social event and many of them couldn't care less about what was going on. They don't even know you're there! The good news was the great press I got, and the reaction of George W. Bush and his wife, Laura — they just loved the show. He was so charming. He has a great sense of humor and he was so friendly. He was so darned nice to me that I couldn't say anything bad about him! You have to be respectful, no matter what your political beliefs are. Ronald

Reagan was the same way, except that he was really liked by most people. His wife, Nancy, was really very nice too. I once played Santa Claus at the White House Christmas party. I got dressed as Santa, and although I knew them very well, she didn't know it was me. She said, 'Who's playing Santa this year?' She took my beard, which was attached by an elastic string, and pulled it down about a foot and let it go, and darn near took my nose off! I met President Nixon a couple of times, and I knew Gerald Ford very well. I've performed for Jimmy Carter and several other presidents, but Reagan was the president I knew best, and I spent a lot of time with him. I met President Clinton in Las Vegas. In Canada, I performed in front of Prime Minister Pierre Trudeau back in the early '70s. He kept asking me if I had any secret information about Frank Sinatra!"

★★★

Rich Little's star continues to shine on the Canadian Walk of Fame in Toronto, along with his three other stars located on the Hollywood, Las Vegas and Palm Springs star-studded Walks of Fame.

It is one of the great pleasures of my life to have been associated with Rich Little over the years, and to have been given the opportunity to contribute on this insightful book.

Raymond Stone
Malibu, California

POST SCRIPT

Can Anyone Be an Impersonator?

*C*an anybody be an impersonator? The answer is yes, but to be good depends how talented they are. Some people *think* they do great impressions, but that's because they can't hear themselves. When I first started out, I had to put everything on a tape recorder and then play it back. That's the only way I knew how it sounded. However, it wasn't long before I developed the ability to hear it as I do it. That's a rare skill. Most people can't do that. They cannot hear themselves.

The most popular voices that people do are John Wayne, Jimmy Stewart, and James Cagney, because they're so much larger than life. A lot of people come up to me and start to do an impression, and I don't know who they're doing. It's very embarrassing. They think it's great; the people around them, friends, relatives, etc., know it's not. These people don't hear themselves, and therefore, don't hear what their impression sounds like.

Can you teach a person to do impressions? Not really, but you can give them suggestive tips: the register's not high enough, or you need more gravel, more bass. The best way to do an impression is to start off with a phrase — something that the celebrity is known for. Clint Eastwood: "Go ahead, make my day," James Cagney: "You dirty rat," and Arnold Schwarzenegger: "I'll be back (Allll be bauk)." If that sounds pretty good, you can go on from there and try daily conversation.

To be a good impersonator, you have to have three things: an interest in people, show business and actors. A good set of vocal cords helps too! A doctor once took a picture of my vocal cords to see if they were any different from anyone else's. Well, they weren't. I think he was expecting to find little people in my throat! My range has always been good. I can do low voices like Orson Welles, Johnny Cash, and John Wayne; as well as the high voices like Jimmie Rodgers, Gene Kelly, and Jimmy Carter.

Believe it or not, singing impressions are the easiest, because you've got the music going for you. If people like the song, and you sound a little like the singer, they'll think it's pretty good.

You can also learn to do impressions by listening and studying other impersonators. You can learn to copy them. I did this when I was younger with George Kirby and Will Jordan. Will Jordan did the best impression ever of Ed Sullivan. He not only sounded like him, he looked like him too. That was a big advantage. All the other impersonators at the time, such as John Byner and Jackie Mason, did their own versions of Ed Sullivan. I've always tried to do an exact copy. To me, that's the definition of an impersonation. If you exaggerate the voice and character like Mason did, then you're doing an impression. It becomes your impression of them, which can be, and often is, an exaggeration. Over the years, I've found that there are more impressionists then impersonators.

Gordie Brown is an impressionist. Gordie is from my home town of Ottawa, Canada. At a very early age, he saw me perform at the National Arts Center in Ottawa, and said to himself, "That's what I want to do – be a mimic like him." I was very flattered when he told me this. When he first came down to Las Vegas from Canada, I used him in a show at the Sahara Hotel called *The Kopykats*. Gordie has gone on to become a very good impressionist and currently has his own show in Las Vegas. However, unlike most of my work, he exaggerates the mannerisms and turns most people he does into a caricature. He is a fabulous entertainer, with fast, rapid-fire delivery. Bill Acosta, who is now retired, and Frankie Scinta both are also very good impressionists. Frankie puts out more energy than the Hoover Dam!

Frankie Scinta, Bill Acosta, Fred Travalena, me,
Bob Anderson & Gordie Brown

I'm of the old school methodology: I set things up and tell jokes. I'm an impersonator. I try to do people exactly how they look and sound. So does Bob

Anderson. He is the best singing impersonator we've ever had. He's recently done a one-man show on Frank Sinatra. It's fantastic! The first time I saw him, I thought he wore too much make up to make him look like Frank. But, he eventually toned it down, and I thought it was much better. I think if you wear too much make up or costuming, you lose your own identity. Fred Travalena, who we lost too soon, was also an impersonator – and a darn good one. He was a wonderful person with a great sense of humor. He was a lot like me and my close friend Steve Rossi, who turned everything we saw or heard into comedy.

I do very few exaggerations. That's why I've done a lot of dubbing in movies, such as when I did David Niven's and Peter Sellers' voices for the *Pink Panther* movies. I've also dubbed for Gene Kelly in a Christmas special when he lost his voice. No one ever knew about these. The producers and actors wanted to keep it quiet. But since they're all gone now, I guess it's okay to talk about it.

My hardest impression was doing Stacy Keach's role as Mike Hammer, when he did the TV show of the same name. He was detained in England, for various reasons, and they needed someone to dub for him in a number of episodes. I had to listen to his voice, quickly record a sentence, listen to his voice again, then record again. It was a tough assignment. I just copied him as best I could. It came off alright, but it was done in bits and pieces.

Special guest Tony Curtis, me & Joe Baker on "The Kopykats": 1972

Tony Curtis once walked off a movie he was doing in Italy, because he wasn't being paid. I didn't know this when the producers came to me and asked if I could dub a few lines of his for this Italian epic. I phoned Tony and told him this. He said, "Don't do it unless you're paid up front." So I did, and they agreed. I phoned Tony back and told him. He said, "If they paid you up front, why didn't they phone and offer it to me!" I said, "Tony, they wouldn't, because they never paid you for the film." He said, "You're right." Then he thought for a moment, and said, "When you get paid, send me the money." "What!" I exclaimed. "Well, you are using my voice!" he replied. Then he thought for a moment longer, and said, "I'm only kidding. Keep the money." To which I replied, "I love you Spartacus."

Jimmy Stewart once said to me, "Rich, I wish I had known you when I was younger; you could've dubbed all my movies for me. Then I could've made a lot more films. The way I talk, it takes me a month to dub one film! Do you know once, I was halfway through making a movie, and I found out they had already completed the sequel?" Everyone has said over the years, that Jimmy hummed and hawed in his movies. But I don't think that's true. He only did that later in life when his memory wasn't as good. He needed time to think about the words, so he got slower and slower as he got older. If you listen to him in *Mr. Smith Goes to Washington,* he actually talks quite fast.

I've always imitated a lot of presidents, because they, too, are larger than life, and have a lot of exposure. Also, people love it when you poke fun at politicians, because they're not usually popular. Older people are also easier to impersonate, because their voices are more distinctive, more mature. Anyone who has a lisp or a raspy voice is also fairly easy to do. I'm always being quoted, when asked who to vote for during election years, that I'm voting for the candidate with the best voice! Who cares what they stand for!

I've always thought doing impressions was a big advantage for me as a comic, because you have two things going for you – the impression and the joke. Sometimes, if the impression is good but the joke is weak, people will still applaud because of the impression. It works the other way around too.

I was in 24 of the 54 *Dean Martin Roasts*. I guess I was asked on so often, not just because my material was pretty good, but mostly because I could imitate a lot of people on the dais. It has always fascinated me that when you imitate someone in front of them, everyone else always looks at the person you're doing to get their reaction. If they react favorably, it means they have a great sense of humor. If not, they're a stuffed shirt. As I stated in the chapter about Paul Lynde, he never liked my impression of him. Every time the camera panned to get his reaction after I did him, it would show Paul laughing. However, that reaction was always taken from another show. He didn't like it at all. Ed Sullivan never liked people impersonating him either. But he realized that if he laughed, it made him look good, so he faked it.

But getting back to can anyone do impersonations or impressions? As I said, yes, they can. It takes a lot of studying, hard work, and perseverance; but if you show any ability at all, just keep at it. However, I'd recommend not trying it out on your family. They tend to be biased. I did impressions for my folks when I was 12. I thought I was hilarious. I wasn't. But, they thought a kid with so much enthusiasm was pretty good, even though I didn't know the names of anyone I was doing!

Strange things people say to me when I'm signing merchandise~

• Fan: My wife thought we were going to see Little Richard!

• Fan: You must be getting on?
Rich: Aren't we all.
Fan: Well, we wanted to catch your show before you died!

• Fan: We met Red Skelton here at this hotel 30 years ago.
Did you know him?
Rich: Yes I did. Did you like him?
Fan: Don't know. We just waved to him!

• Fan: You didn't do my favorite actor tonight.
Rich: Who was that?
Fan: Van Johnson!

• Fan: I enjoyed your show.
You know, you dated my mother years ago. She's a big fan.
Rich: What's her name? Is she here?
Fan: Her name's Janet. And no she's not here.
She's not in very good shape.
Rich: Sorry to hear that.
Fan: Well, she *is* in her 90s!

• Fan: Was this the same show we saw 30 years ago at the Sahara Hotel?

• Fan: I'm from Canada. We were in the same grade at
Glebe Collegiate.
Rich: I didn't go to Glebe Collegiate.
Fan: Yes, you did!

• 15 yr. old boy: I enjoyed your show. You were very funny.
But just one thing puzzles me.
Rich: What was that?
Boy: Why did you keep changing your voice?

ABOUT THE AUTHOR

*R*ICH LITTLE is an internationally known impersonator and master of mimicry.

Known as the *Man of 200 Voices,* he has appeared on television and stage for over five decades, entertaining audiences and making them laugh. He is one of only a select few to have stars on all four Walks of Fame: Canada, Hollywood, Las Vegas and Palm Springs. He is currently performing "Rich Little Live!" in Las Vegas, as well as touring around the country. He is currently launching his newly self-written show "Little by Little," an autobiographical trip down memory lane with familiar voices and vintage video, in the hopes of a Broadway run.

This is his first book and has enjoyed all the experiences of working with the celebrities written about.

He was born in Ottawa, Canada, but now resides in Las Vegas, Nevada.